MATURE MASCULINITY

Man's Inner Essence

Brian,

Thanks for your thoughtful engagement

Sujith

MATURE MASCULINITY

Man's Inner Essence

Sujith Ravindran

Published by

MELROSE BOOKS

An Imprint of Melrose Press Limited
St Thomas Place, Ely
Cambridgeshire
CB7 4GG, UK
www.melrosebooks.com

FIRST EDITION, 2011

Publication of
BLUE TEMPLE ACADEMY
www.bluetempleacademy.com

ISBN 978 1 907732 64 5

Printed and bound in Great Britain by:
CPI Group (UK) Ltd, Croydon, CR0 4YY

"Kshanta hao go pita Shivananda ar sahé na
Kuver yar bhandari Brahma Vishnu dvarer dvari.
Ami tanri ajinakari jereo ki ta jana na."[9]

[I am a follower of Shiva,
the brilliance of whose divine presence outshines even the dazzling brilliance of the jewels of *Kubera's* (the mythological treasurer of heaven) treasury;
whose unmatched dexterity in creation excels even that of the creator *Brahma* himself;
whose unequalled love surpasses even that of the preserver *Vishnu* himself;
In whose loving shelter not only humans, but also animals and plants feel absolutely secure.]

ACKNOWLEDGEMENTS

During my childhood, numerous teachers, preachers, town folks and relatives shared their glorious stories of Shiva, the Indian god of consciousness, with me. Many of you recited verses after verses of feats of Shiva, instilling in that child in me a sense of awe and disbelief towards this Almighty Being. Lots of what I learned came every evening through the loud conical speakers of the temple around the corner which blared the glory and greatness of Shiva. Memories of the town folks who incessantly chanted, all night long, the melodious poems from the ancient texts during the festival evenings still remain with me. Parents and relatives put me to sleep often nights narrating stories of Shiva's victories over evil and darkness. Comic books with their gripping pictures and lofty narratives created a great fascination and deep learning in me for the splendour of that *Maha Purush* (Great Being), Shiva. I can never thank enough all of you who can take credit for this work.

Further, my heartfelt gratitude goes to Dada Shambhushivananda and his trainee monks (at the Centre For Neohumanist Studies in Ydrefors, Sweden) for creating a space of grace for me to finalize this book. Without your amazing devotion, love and selfless service, I would never have been able to so effortlessly open my inner most doors and connect with my innermost voice. Every impression gathered, every sentence read, every word exchanged, every moment of meditation with you at the Centre was a fountain of inspiration for me.

Over the years, many coaching clients have come as blessings into my life through my seminars and workshops, but also in one-on-one settings. Not only have you all illuminated the highest truth in man in your own life journeys, but also through your passion and radiance, you have gifted yourselves as shining examples to those in your lives. You have been such a blessing to me as well in my journey of anchoring myself deeper in my own experience of the amazing power of the mature masculine.

I also wish to acknowledge you, mom, for having given the space to your less-than-ideal son to expand into his 'real' self, and for having weathered many storms to realize the meaning of your human existence.

To Mark Vandeneijnde for your priceless friendship through the times before and during the conception and creation of this work; to Anja Hulskotter for your noble example of life, and your passion that is pure and awesome; to Michiel ten Kate for your exuberance and spirit of transformation. Your much valued outlook and your meticulous and critical remarks on the first draft helped me bring in meaning, richness, and give a consistent form and shape to this text.

Finally, thank you, all my readers. By choosing to gift yourselves the reminder of the truths of the Mature Masculine, you have taken the time to refresh yourselves of what you already knew; you have had the feeling for the Mature Masculine, within yourselves or within your partner, family, friends, colleagues or other acquaintances, and which had temporarily been outside your present consciousness. Man by man, we can help men come back home to their mature masculine selves and live their fullest joy.

I dedicate this book to all those men who yearn to come home to their Mature Masculine self.

TABLE OF CONTENTS

1. PREFACE

We live in a world where when society refers to masculinity, it means an adolescent form of rough rugged expression of man. In my numerous conversations with (mostly western) men and women alike, I have noticed masculinity being associated with 'macho' and aggression, the end result being that any association with masculinity seems to have become anathema in society's eyes. This collective (self) condemnation has pushed masculine expression to the dark cellars of men's personalities, chained to be imprisoned forever in many cases. I myself was stuck in this trap for a while, imagining naively that it is for me to be someone who I am not, or risk being ostracized. When I became aware of my victim hood, and the low potential that my life yielded, I recognized that at the risk of being non-conformist, I must find myself, at least my most authentic human self. Thus began this cycle of self-discovery that has led to this book.

This book is not an intellectual exercise, rather an extraction of the lessons I learned in the course of discovering my own mature masculine self. Though this book explores masculinity in the context of man's modern life, it does bring a certain understanding of the feminine as well, due to the polar nature of both sexes. It is quite difficult to treat the subject of masculinity in isolation, separate from femininity; as challenging as it is to capture the fullness of Shiva's immanence without capturing the energy of *Shakti* (the divine feminine force of creation). However, I have chosen to treat the interplay between the mature masculine and the feminine in a sequel.

All the masculine attributes and qualities that I expand upon in the subsequent pages come from the eminent personality of Shiva or from His revered teachings. In here, there is no allusion to god or religion, for that would only limit the infinite degrees of freedom possessed by the mind to expand man in consciousness. References to the ancient texts are included in order to enrich the intuitive learning of the reader, and anchor the essence of the subject in that of Shiva's truth. The content herein is not based upon theological reasoning of life, but on the experience of spiritual life; man's highest, most fulfilling, most meaningful essence of living. It finds its origin in the ancient spirit of India, that which still manifests in modern Indian life; generations of men find their life's fulfilment by making living use of this spirit that is very native to all. Thus the text has been written with modern man in mind, but it offers infinite degrees of freedom for man to apply it in ways which suit him best, for we are all the same as we are different.

The Mature Masculine is the embodiment of man's highest ideal, the essence of Shiva that lies within all men. This ideal is not a faraway concept, witnessed in history books or epics, out of reach of the men of today; rather it is that which is innate to every man, rearing its head every day in tiny ways, glimpsing the light for moments each day. It is in the embodiment of this ideal that man finds himself in full alignment with all there is, and be able to access all his potentialities, and express his full potential. However varied his life today is from the days of the past, the ancient essence is still applicable to his modern life; the deepest essence of man has not changed, for it is not preordained to change.

I have composed this work not out of arrogance of how well I know Shiva or the mythology surrounding him, but out of admiration; nor have I written it from a self-endowed moral high ground, but from a place of humility; and not out of cold intellect, but out of devotion. It is a hard job trying to deconstruct a god, but I seek consolation in the fact that Shiva was a human being who lived his most divine attributes.

The usage of the masculine gender in the text is not meant to confine its message solely to the male among us. The usage of the masculine is purely meant as a literature style, and to keep the focus on the masculine core that resides within both man and woman.

It is my deepest yearning that the man of today will see that he is not **in** light, that he is more; he is **of** light, for such is his divinity. When he recognizes that consciousness has evolved through eons, having found its expression in atoms, then molecules, then unicellular beings, then multi-cellular beings, then plants, then animals, until consciousness has found expression in him, then he realizes the supreme within him. Of all of creation, he is of the highest consciousness, standing on the final step of this magnificent cycle of evolution, poised to merge back into the eternal bliss of *Parama Purusha* (Supreme Consciousness) again.

A teacher once reminded me that, for each man, the next message of transformation is waiting around the corner. It could be hidden in a sign from nature, or within the lines in an article, or in the words spoken by another, or hiding behind an inner door awaiting its turn to be opened. All it takes man is to open his eyes and reach out and receive it. It is my earnest intention for each reader that at least one chapter contained herein will resonate with him or her. If I can accomplish that, I would consider my duty fulfilled.

Each chapter tackles one attribute of Shiva, an attribute that bring out the Mature Masculine's shine and glitter. At the end of each chapter a list of questions are provided for the reader to reflect and meditate upon in his own process of uncovering that attribute, that which is already residing within. This work is not written for easy reading, but for patient assimilation. It is through such dissemination that the full impact of the text can be availed in the lives of both men and women. With that request, I invite men to read this book with their entire being, while I invite women to read it with their divine empathetic radar of understanding the other gender. I also invite you to share your thoughts at www.maturemasculinity.net, to help me illuminate my life with learning, and to encourage my daily practice of living my highest ideal.

Sujith Ravindran
October 2010.

2. INTRODUCTION

"Thus the pilgrimage in the outer space is actually the mirrored reflection of an inner movement or development, directed towards a yet unknown distant aim which, however, is intrinsically and seed-like contained in the very direction of that movement. Here from springs the readiness to cross the horizons of the known and the familiar, the readiness to accept people and new environments as parts of our destiny, and the confidence in the ultimate significance of all that happens and is in harmony with the depth of our being and the universality of a greater life."

(Anagarika Govinda)

* * * * * * * *

As I huddled next to my backpack aboard the bus to Tawaghat, a small Himalayan village, my heart remained filled with questions, timeless questions that have found not their resolution. I felt as if my being was the confluence of many magical lifetimes and roles, and my intellect was voicing to me the truth underlying my existence; that the longing of the self was to be in union with the Self, that in this union resides the expression of my most mature masculine nature that I longed to own and embrace. Many have walked this path before me; many have undertaken this quest, seeking to find the radiance of their spirit within, which is man's highest nature, the oneness which illuminates the path of his life.

I felt restless, my inner dialogue incessant and the questions ceaseless; perhaps because I have been 'given' until the 13th sunrise to show my presence at the door of the hermit again.

* * * * * * * *

As I greeted the hermit respectfully with a slight bow, with my hands pressed together, palms touching and fingers pointed upwards, in front of my chest, I asked him, "Guruji, what is it to be a man?"

No answer came my way as his piercing eyes continued being fixed at me. For a moment I assumed that he did not grasp my question, however I saw in his eyes that he did. So I expanded my query, "What is the experience of being man?"

* * * * * * * *

My encounter with this hermit at Dharchula, a Himalayan village, was the culmination of my travails through various Indian states, visiting the most erudite and divine among men as there could ever be.

Man violates integrity when he underutilizes his infinite potential, for man is preordained to uphold his personal, social and spiritual pacts; each time he shirks away from his *Dharma* (purpose of being), he makes the burden heavier on Nature's shoulder, he exists upon the barren grounds where love sprouts not, and he lives in bankruptcy of the incessant joy he is designed for.

For each man who is steeped in the life of utility, there is another who seeks to transcend the worldly to access that which is greater in him. Among the latter, I found many who have ceded their hearts to be completely occupied by Shiva, He who is believed to be capable of providing the whole universe to the man who devotes himself to Him. Ranging from the south of India to the north, from the erudite to the practical, from the purely dogmatic to the purely rational, these devotees of Shiva lived in *Seva* (selfless service to all beings), for in the very act of *Seva* lies the path that merges the principles and the personality.

I served and lived in the company of erudite men who imparted the principles that come out of the life and teachings of Shiva, both mythological and real; they pour generously out of the cauldron of wisdom from which has risen the awakening of millions. Some recognize Shiva as part of a broader range of principles that govern the universe, while others focus on the experience of Shiva as part of their inner being; that beings are all the same thing, composed of infinite and inexhaustible life.

Devotees who take the alternate route of practice and rituals go by the belief that the essence of Shiva - with his infinite wisdom and love - is present within all beings, animate and inanimate, and man's daily *Sadhana* (spiritual practice) is to access and experience that inner essence which is greater than his human self, the essence that is unlimited and unconfined within the physical shell. I joined them in their ancient shamanistic rituals that synthesize the body and mind experiences to achieve alternative levels of reality; rituals devised to help man transcend the realm of space and time, and slip into the subtle non-physical experience of egolessness, surrender, communion with the Absolute, and thence blissful delirium. These men have embraced a level of disqualification of the socially-accepted norms and rituals, to adopt a life of renunciation of the worldly existence.

Certain schools of *Tantra* teach man to respect all the different archetypes in man that are real, that he holds within him the duality of the spirit that shines forth in its unconditional love, as well as the dark forces that limit him to his sensorial pursuit. To resolve this duality and fuse him into the oneness that he truly is, these teachings sanctify the dark forces, and integrate them into rituals that are believed to take man towards greater self-realization. Such *Tantrics* (one who practices *Tantra*) step into the practice of sexual experiences beyond the ordinary, they indulge the stomach, they engage in intoxication, and wield personal power.

Many paths, all meant to lead to one destination; self-realization.

*   *   *   *   *   *   *   *

For many decades, this hermit has been a devotee of Shiva, He who is known as the embodiment of the noblest within man. In worship of Shiva lives a whole town called Bageshwar, not far from where this hermit lived, for in Bageshwar humanity finds its deepest connection with the truth and spirit of Shiva. He who is in pursuit of self-realization, he who seeks his non-physical and physical dissolution in the truest that lives within him, his journey is incomplete if he has not stopped and spent time in Bageshwar; hence I arrived in Bageshwar. On my third day, word of this hermit from Dharchula fell upon my ears.

As I stood in his presence, I felt humbled by his shine and simplicity. His whose face I was staring at was not a plain one, but it was very handsome, and it was enigmatic. His piercing eyes gave a look which no man could sustain without emotion, and spellbound under it, I stood transfixed.

Amidst his wild shaggy beard, greyed from every angle, his lips were settled into a relaxed but determined curve. He was dressed in saffron, the harmony of his colours broken only by the faded deep purple cardigan that protected his frail body from the chill. He was seated on a wooden stool barely fifteen centimetres off the veranda, his legs crossed, his arms resting on his laps facing upwards. His spine was erect and rested against the back drop of a greyish brown clay wall, with the door to his cottage open into what seemed like endless dark inside. His cottage was made of thatched leaves, and the fragrance of sandalwood hung in the air, the only sound I could hear was the occasional shout of children playing somewhere down in the valley.

I observed a man of great eccentricity of character, who, having taken up his abode in this place remote, contented himself with a solitary life, in the company of flora and fauna that rested in the same quiet that he was composed of. From him emanated a constant hum of devotional chant of Shiva, which gave an added éclat to his hermit-like appearance.

As I looked at him expectantly, he beckoned me with a swing of his left hand to sit down. I sat down on the cold floor of the veranda, careful not to have my feet pointing at him. Silence spoke louder than words, as a slight smile steeped in understanding appeared on his face; he nodded his head as if in some cosmic conversation with an unknown being deep within me.

“So you are here.” He finally spoke. Then after a pause he continued, “Yada vabhavyamasti”. I knew it meant ‘whatever will be, will be’ in Sanskrit.

As silence spread its wings again, he asked me, “Can you define love for me?”

After a thoughtful minute, I hesitantly replied, "I am not sure I can offer you a good definition of love, but I know it when I feel love in me.”

He continued looking at me. I could see his eyes speak, as he turned his gaze into the woods behind me. His left hand slowly moved towards his beard, stroking it, as his gaze rested back upon me. “Can you define the soul to me?” He asked.

I simply looked at him in silence, for what I must leave unsaid there is no substitute to fill with; words felt to me like a mere makeshift arrangement.

Then he asked, "Can you define consciousness for me?" The questions felt rhetorical to me.

As I sat there, I felt a bond of harmony between us, a harmony of thoughts that which made us act in unison. In our moment of seeker and teacher, there existed no confusion.

He went silent again, eyes closed, as quiet as the setting around us felt. It was late afternoon, but the light was fading. Various thoughts appeared to me as I contemplated the answers to his questions, the inquisitive man within me was searching the connection between love, soul and consciousness, for all that is real for man has its oneness at the primordial level. I felt there must be some connection between his questions which was not apparent to me yet. So I decided to wait for him to open his eyes.

In the space of allowing, man fuses into Nature, time melts into timelessness, 'doing' and 'being' becomes one, thoughts merge into the space between thoughts. I felt as if the answers to my questions, the truths of my quests, were near, it was presenting itself in its natural elements, and all I needed was to reach out and grab it from the space around me. I was reminded of this hermits first words, 'whatever will be, will be.'

After what seemed like minutes, he opened his eyes and spoke, "Walk alone to the Om Parvat, offer your prayers at the seat of Shiva at Parvati Sarovar, and be here on the 13th sunrise." Om Parvat is a mountain in the Himalayas.

He shut his eyes again. As I sat there watching him, I felt a sudden shiver run down my spine, excitement coursed through my blood, as with one who awaits judgment day. The truth that lies within, longing to burst forth and shine in all its glory, was it seeking its expression through the directive of this aged man who has dedicated his life in pursuit of his worldly liberation? I could hardly formulate words in my own mind, for a great love and a great dread had seized upon me at once, nevertheless I could feel I was close to the revelation of my truth.

* * * * * * * *

Tawaghat is the point of confluence of two rivers, one of which carries a black hue about its water, its big black rocks carrying a shiny tone. As I headed out on the trail alongside the river, I found myself talking to myself. All of that which was roaming as thoughts within me, all my inner dialogues, they were finding their expression in my verbalization. The air felt fresh and warm, only punctuated by an occasional breeze which gave me a slight chill.

It is said in the ancient texts that the primordial sound 'Om' is the bow, the *Atman* (the individual soul) is the arrow and *Paramatman* (the Universal Soul) the target. As my whole being permeated with fresh energy, and my mind tuned into my purpose, I felt that I was the arrow. Confined within this human act of trekking, or in the destination of this effort, lies the release on man's inner essence. Why else was such renunciation a common ritual of so many who have found release from the bondages of the mind?

As the afternoon wore down so did my inner dialogue. The loud voices bellowing within me, the anxiety that crowded me as I headed into Tawaghat, all of that started to finds its replacement in silence. My verbal dialogue was replaced by a gentle hum of tunes that stuck with me from the past weeks.

As I walked into Sirkha, villagers greeted me with their customary, but warm and genuine 'Om namah Shivaya' (hallowed be Shiva's name), as is their usual practice with visitors. But without wasting a moment, I continued walking past the little town to arrive at the next village, for I felt energized in the abundance of my love, love for the act of searching for that which is dearest to my being. At the outskirts of the village I pitched tent for the night, stretched myself, and sunk into a deep meditation. As I sat there, the vision of a bright light flashed on my inner eye, and it dawned to me that only in this deep state of 'being' does my being find its reconciliation with my 'doing', for that communion is my *Sadhana* (spiritual practice).

My next two days were most scenic as well as risky; it was forever uphill as I trekked alongside the River Kali. Like the variant colours of peacock feathers, Nature offered me a bouquet of beautiful waterfalls, glaciers, lush green valleys, sparkling water, tall dense trees, flowers and white peaks. Life's questions alternately swirled and settled within me, continuing their periodic dance, and I observed myself becoming the witness of my inner reality. At one moment I felt centred, the debacles of worldly life seeming insignificant, my truth liberated and whole, the next moment I sighed in discontent and weariness of failure. On occasions my vast bottomless spirit rejoiced in my equanimity and oneness with the glorious moments unfolding within and around me, on others my shallow heart slumped into regrets of the past and anxieties for the future. Tears, as forceful as the waters of the river I walked alongside, burst forth and streamed down my face, sobs escaped my being as faces from my past flashed before my eyes and pain gripped my heart; as the burden of my deeds was replaced by the compassionate observer within me, my heart emerged crystal clear and light, with a stability and forbearance about me.

In the serene depth of my mind, I felt the same energy which vibrates and passes through the endless forms of Nature.

Goodness is the true nature of humanity, goodness that shines when man is free from his fears; like the blossoms in the valley when the sun is out, goodness was abundant in the villages I passed. In their love and kindness, the villagers had no hesitation in acknowledging their kinship with Nature, for they were fully alive to Nature. They had established a conscious relationship with it, not merely out of greed for Nature's offerings, but truly realizing it in their spirit of connection.

I pitched tent once next to a military camp. In man's principle-centeredness, in his noble encounter with adversity, can be seen the divine nature of his masculine essence, for it makes more of man, not lesser. That was evident in these tough and hostile conditions, where the military men were impelled by their duty, but that did not diminish their cordiality and humility. I stood witness to the dignity of their being, their sacrifice being its own legacy, more supreme than any saintly man's pilgrimage.

Like melody originates from the coupling of the low note with the high note, wild nature's harmony resides in every steep climb followed by a downhill run. I take a turn and suddenly I stumble upon a gushing stream, or brush against a bush of tiny flowers growing on rocks, birds of exotic nature nonchalantly pass in proximity, Nature looks back at me benignly through its mountain peaks and valleys. I stood there momentarily basking in my experience of liberation, until that moment was taken over by guilt; guilt for having excused myself from my assigned place in the grind. How do I justify my escape from the routine enforced upon me by the collective ego of society? The noble within man has reminded him time and again that there was neither beauty nor joy in living for its own sake, but that he must live to serve himself and the Infinite through his service of humanity. As I lay witness to this truth, into my fourth day in wilderness, the inner tug-of-war persisted, liberation and guilt in warfare.

I was told that I could have my first glimpse of the Om Parvat the next day. I paused occasionally for breath, keeping my break short for fear of relaxing my muscles and losing body warmth. My mind impelled me through its anticipation, thoughts were far and few, but questions about my destination were aplenty, rising frequently like a lashing wave and receding again. "Why am I here", I asked myself. I did not consider myself overly religious or dogmatic, but there was a part of me that proclaimed that man must follow his most divine inner voice, for in its calling lies the key to his greatest pursuit, liberation. At that moment, as I stood there with the wind against my face, I felt I was living in honour of my most divine inner voice.

As I walked by, I noticed many tilted houses - like caricatures made of cardboard boxes in some film set - in the village of Garbyang. They all seemed uninhabited; seemingly since next to this desolate hutment stood a village with life visible. The village was also the point of confluence of two rivers one of which was the black water of Kali. Nature's miracle makes the water flow, for if those rivers were to standstill, all that would be visible to man's eyes is ice. For the first time, here I crossed the River Kali, my companion for the past four days.

For the first time in four days, I spoke to another of the purpose of my trip, a secret that was this far deep held within

me. As the words poured out of me, the truth of my own pursuit started to become more vivid, for only in the presence of innocence can man see the most obvious.
"What will you find at Om Parvat?" I was asked in broken English by a young man. "I don't know," I responded with a smile. "Perhaps a book with all the secrets of what it means to be a man." As I spoke those words, we both broke into laughter.

In his presence, I discovered that what I must find, must I find within. There is only so much that any external source can offer man, that which can open an inner door. But that which is true to man must be found within, for man's truth resides within. As I shared my thoughts about my inner quest with the young man, I was confronted by a blank stare.

Villagers stepped forward as I bid them farewell, many advised me to use the accompaniment of a pony or a porter; I declined, for this was my rite of passage, the rite that I must undertake alone. I felt elated, here I am almost in sight of my physical destination, and resounding within me was my truth seeking its realization. I could feel its yearning to surface into my consciousness, I could feel it because forgiveness was coming easy to me. Those with whom I felt trapped with for years through my judgment were arousing only compassion within me. I felt benevolent in my love for them.

As I walked along the prettiest of Nature's manifestations, the most scenic of meadows that I have laid eyes upon, towards my right I saw the Om Parvat mountain sticking out over the clouds, with its unmistakable 'ॐ' shaped glacier upon it. I stood there in amazement, for Nature was not only a creator, but also undoubtedly an artist; that no measure of man's creativity could conceive such an invention, simple in its art, majestic in its articulation.

That evening, I decided to set up camp not far from the holy temple of Goddess Kali and Lord Shiva in Kalapani, the origin of River Kali. As I refreshed myself in the inn at the premises of the temple, I came across a group of Shaivaite (devotees of Shiva) pilgrims on their way back from the Om Parvat. I felt drawn to their asceticism and simple-heartedness, so I joined them in their evening prayers, meditation, chanting and practice of Thandhava (the dance of Shiva).

The whole group hopped the Thandava to the beats of the *Acharya* (the teacher), as he bellowed the rhythm "Ta ta thing ta" as he violently clapped his hands together while dancing himself. I joined the group in their dance as they responded to the rhythm at the top of their lungs with "thing thing thing ta".

And so it continued,
"Ta ta thing ta"
"Thing thing thing ta"

As I started to gasp for breath, the teacher raised the tempo, and I could notice the veins protruding from his neck, his face turning red through his shaggy beard, spit flying out of his mouth, as he ground the words out. Fire was coming out of his eyes, and the *Rudraksh* (a beaded chain) around his neck was being thrown around, slapping his grey beard with every hop. I danced mesmerized as I noticed the transcendence of the whole group into some alternate plane. The teacher was in delirium, absent from his physical reality as brute force exuded from his self, as I became the witness of his primal expression, lost in a trance, completely oblivious of his physical setting.

I felt a strange primal energy awaken within me, seeking to burst forth, and as I struggled to fall in line with the beats, I could feel the energy in the room overpower me. All I could see was men in sweat, my ears reverberating with the teacher's loud "Ta ta thing ta" followed by the screams of "Thing thing thing ta" from the followers. The hurt in my knees that I have been feeling since the previous day started to disappear as if I did not own my knees anymore, my hops started to become effortless as a heady lightness started to envelop me. Like a tennis ball, I was hopping off the floor as my chants were no longer a conscious effort; it came out of some inner place, deep within, as I felt a witness to another being within me chanting on my behalf.

"Ta ta thing ta, thing thing thing ta", the chant continued, as it was getting more and more distant to me until it became a faint buzz in the background as I felt my body bounce off the floor. I was overcome by delirium, a strange ease enveloped me as I felt myself lost in an ecstatic abandon. I felt my face explode into a big smile; the physical reality was distant to me.

The next day was my anticipated day of arrival at Om Parvat. I pushed myself along the northwest trail, climbing with panting breath in the rarefied air of the high altitude, passing forests of deodar trees, with their neatly trimmed looks, respecting each other's space even as they co-existed together in wilderness. En route I crossed a few glaciers, battling the wind against my face, as I admired the picturesque, soul-touching view around. My mind was in quietness; thoughts were few and rare, and the silence between my thoughts stretched further and further. In that peace appeared an inexplicable joy, as I stood silently in the presence of Om Parvat.

Though the temperature dipped to freezing with high velocity wind, the skies held clear, as if in waiting for me, as I stood there counting my blessings for the clear view of the mountain peak. Oblivious to the dipping mercury and the blowing winds, I stood there gazing at the peak unblinkingly, letting myself be enveloped by a deep sense of fulfilment, the fulfilment that comes from the communion of desire and its object. In that moment, I saw no birds or butterflies, no trees or flowers, no other mountains or streams, the rest of the world felt opaque to me. I felt humbled into a speck in the enormity of creation, I felt insignificant in the presence of its might, with its great height, sheer beauty and its awesome power. In that insignificance, I felt complete, the completeness of being a woven part of a whole.

It is believed in mythology that Parvati, Shiva's consort, spent many years in penance here to attain the love of Shiva. Lake Parvati, at the base of Om Parvat, reflected the sight and soul of the mountain peak, bringing to equality all that is created by the same hands.

When man has curbed himself from the full realization of the divine in humanity, his aspiration cannot go beyond the idea of success, and his walls are built around him not beyond his life of sensorial pursuit or mere necessity. An illusory vision of immortality and omnipotence impels such man to latch on to the false notion of grandiose. However, when he is viewed through the reflection in the lake, he is lower than the rest. He has failed in his ambition to look greater in the eyes of the witness who chooses to watch only his reflection. Thus the Lake Parvati stood for the metaphor for the very antithesis of all that man considers mighty.

That afternoon I made a *Parikrama* (circumambulation) of the lake. Standing next to the lake was the shrine of Shiva and Parvati that the hermit had asked of me to visit. As I sat next to the shrine, I felt the divinity of the spot. If man's quest is for an unconditional life, he need not look further, for here there was no hierarchy, all beings – animate and inanimate – were designed as equal, and this spot stood as a museum of that truth. As I looked east I noticed a pair of swans float through the sky, over the distant green and the snowy plateaus, heading in my direction. As I sat there admiring the beauty of Nature's parade of its most priceless, the swans glided through the air, and landed on the lake. I was informed that the pair arrived from Manasa Sarovar, another lake in the Tibetan Himalayas, located at the base of Mount Kailash, the mythological abode of Shiva. In mythology it is believed that these swans are not mere birds, instead the embodiment of none other than Shiva and his consort, Parvati. I felt the thrill of being the momentary witness of a cosmic conspiracy unfolding on the silver screen of Nature in front of me. In that moment, all functions and dysfunctions, all positives and negatives, all good and evil, all merged into perfection.

As I prepared to turn back after my second night by the Om Parvat, I sunk into confusion. I was unable to understand the whys and wherefores, and I wondered what was I doing there? What was the lesson hidden here for me? What was the revelation for me from this setting that radiated its magnificence in unspoken words? Was this trip preordained for something larger than myself that my ego, in its narrow limited self, failed to grasp, or was this trip my naïve attempt to take over all the pains and sufferings and misfortunes of the world, under the illusion that I was the next cross bearer who will bear it and bring it over to the Supreme?

As I started my trek back to Gunji, the awareness dawned upon me that my greatest practice in dealing with my questions was one of detaching myself from all self-enhancing outcomes, that this is a matter of choice. That I was the choice-maker within the limits of the preordained path scripted for me, and that I reserved the choice of progressing towards the Absolute or retreating on that path away from the Absolute. In my receptivity towards the Infinite could I read the signs and access the answers that served my path.

It was my ninth morning on the trail, and I started to notice the hurt on my right knee, which got worse after every break I took. At Gunji, I received some herbal medication to be packed around my knee. With the increasing pain also went up my determination to make it back to the hermit within the committed time. Part of me spoke that mastering my pain was a component of my rite of passage, and it was my duty to penetrate the pain to access the peace that resided within all pain. I had to stay with the pain, not deny it. I had to get intimate with it, like I had to permit my emotional pain come close to me, in that would I find my release.

Some eight kilometres from Budhi, I decided to lighten my load, so I left behind my butane burner, the two utensils and the ready-to-cook canned items I carried. I wrapped the food tightly in a polythene bag and placed everything carefully on a ledge next to the trail, hoping that some other pilgrim would make use of them. The offloading felt like a symbolic expression of the spiritual truth in man; renunciation. Faced with the adversities of life, like petals from an aging flower falling away, all wants peel off, and at the elemental level man reaches a place where only the bare necessities matter. What felt relevant at a physical and physiological level, is no more within the sphere of concern of man. His reference for life transcends the physical to embrace the metaphysical, references that were ephemeral become eternal. I knew that my journey back to where I started would unquestionably reach its fruition without the extra provisions and gear.

I felt I could use the comfort of a bed, and the space to set my belongings. Above all, I felt like saving the effort of pitching and dismantling the tent, and resting my knee in comfort, so I checked into the government public works rest house in Malpa, next to which, on my way up, I had pitched my tent. Unlike the last time, this time I felt my soul soar in freedom in my choice of not being in isolation, for freedom lies in the choices of man to commit. The opposites can both lead to the exact same experience of freedom in man, for the spirit in which the self merges in freedom is the same; that real freedom is of the spirit, it can never come to man from outside.

And the spirit, in experiencing its freedom, wants to explore, wants to see everything, wants to listen to every sound, and wants to smell every flower in Nature. It wants to rejoice in its infinite joy as it splashes in the water in every stream, and though limited in my capacity to choose for the spirit, I allow it to live its truest longing.

As the weather turned wet and windy, the trail got trickier to navigate with the snow storm blowing rashly by. Unlike the higher altitudes of the previous few days, breathing was easier, a joyful recompense for the inclement weather. The storm stinging my face was an even sweeter distraction from my hurting knee, another one of the countless designs of Nature to carry me in its cradle from beginning to the end of this trip.

Past Malpa and down and down towards Galagad alongside the River Kali, with my heart choking, both from the searing pain in my knees and from the intensity of the catharsis, I felt caught up in the raw energy of the wilderness surrounding me. I was being carried in a trance as I descended step by step, with the chant of 'Om Namah Shivaya' (hallowed be Shiva's name) leading me deeper into the trance. I recognized that I had crossed the passage of life that took me into the realm of 'allowing'.

I came across a group headed in the opposite direction towards Mount Kailash, the mythological abode of Shiva; some seated on ponies, some walking, all chanting in gusto devotional songs and mantras of Shiva. As I approached the group, one of the porters leaned forward and handed me a herbal ball, and upon inspection I discovered that it was cannabis leaves, growing lushly on both sides of the trail. I politely declined with a smile, handed the ball back to him and wishing them well on their trip. I felt that I did not need any intoxicating agent, that the bliss that I experienced at that moment was unsurpassable.

However, that was not to be so. The afternoon turned pleasant, a warm sun beating down upon me, a gentle breeze blowing in the opposite direction, the landscape studded with waterfalls, and the path weaving through a vibrantly rich valley; all an enervating delight for tired eyes. Nature's music was on, birds were singing and the River Kali's crackle, splash and rumble filled the space.

With the sun also came the flies, they were everywhere. They buzzed, and the buzz felt welcoming in the beginning until the flies were in my ears, they were in my eyes, they were inside my long johns. My bliss was slowly being replaced by irritation, for any sensation that is dependent upon man's external setting is as transient as the setting itself. The swift change in my state of mind questioned the true nature of the joy that I was feeling. Was the joy that I was feeling earlier through the day truly anchored in my inner core or was it attached to something external to me?

That which was all beauty and joy-evoking was instantly replaced with a reality filled with a hurting knee, annoying flies, soaked and sore outfit, and an endless trail. Rage appeared at the victim hood I felt. That was my response to the experience that I had to comply to, which felt a violation of my pact with the Absolute. I entered a lower plane of awareness, a plane that was filled with my anger of having to comply against my will, and the exasperation of being condemned for who I felt I am. I let the anger course through my being, letting it flow through my whole body, having every cell awash by it. The whole setting seemed unfair, the whole deal an injustice as I trudged step by step down the trail, cursing for having to be careful with each step on the slippery slope.

As I settled down at the military camp near Sirkha, so did the anger within. What answer, I asked, do I give to the questions my anger raises? As I slipped into the silence of meditation, wrapped in a warm blanket and sitting at the isolated end of a long veranda, the message of my anger appeared as the traumas that lie within the inner life of self. Its origin lay, it felt, in the break of harmony with the love within me, some disconnect from the forgiveness that lie abundantly within. I felt drained, but the truth also served me peace within myself.

I started early on the last day of my trek to Tawaghat, the village where the trek began. It was still dawn, the light down, the sun yet to appear. It was meant to be a clear day, free of clouds and rain, and I knew the right thing to do was to drag my inflamed knee at a gentle pace, without long breaks, profusely applying the ointment graciously offered by the military men of this little Himalayan village called Sirkha that I might never visit again in this lifetime. I carried the precious ointment close to my heart, but closer remained my profound gratitude for those men who silently lived their missions in a service greater than their limited human selves. As I continued on my descent back into the relative plains, I was filled with gratitude; gratitude to be chosen to undertake this trip, gratitude for all the events past that have shaped me to be who I was at that moment, gratitude for being called upon so early in this lifetime to find my truth, and the greatest source of gratitude being the hour I get to spend in my window of life after each day's dissipation is all over.

My legs were wobbly, but they carried upon them the undying spirit that expressed its life through me. Tears streamed down my face as I walked in awareness that I was blessed, that my distance from my truth might be unfathomable, for distance cannot be estimated in cosmic measures, but the distance that I have covered felt immense. Life felt perfect, for all that is mundane in life holds perfection, that perfection is not a virtue limited to royal splendour. Paradise was what man chooses to make of it, the shining example of which I witnessed during my days in those remote mountainous villages. The villagers have found their perfection in their hearts through the kinship they felt with the woodland, the mountains, the streams, the snow, and all beings – animate and inanimate, for perfection comes from oneness, the oneness that makes them more than the sum of each individual part. What was lesser in them in their worldly roles was more than compensated with more in soul, their forbearance as plentiful as the deodar trees in the Himalayan forests, their serene strength compounded with their humility and benevolence, their ascetic purity of love expressing itself through their simple-heartedness and playful approach to life. Each time when I saw them stand up and beckon the pilgrims with the authentic intimacy of kindred, they filled me with great joy and a high hope for humanity's ultimate union with the Absolute.

As I was walking up to the cottage of the hermit, I felt an intense energy coursing through me and filling my being with an intense knowingness. I could not place a finger upon my knowingness, yet at a subtle level I felt the essence of what it meant crossing the limiting barriers of the individual and be greater than who I was in my human form; my inner experience was not grandiose or dressed in splendour, rather I felt awash in a serene joy.

He was seated at the exact same spot where I found him thirteen days ago, dressed in the same outfit that I saw him in the last time, his face radiated the same expression as before, and he observed me with the same piercing look as when I first met him.

As I stood there in his presence, he beckoned me with a swing of his left hand to sit down. I sat down on the cold floor of his veranda, at the exact spot where I was seated thirteen days ago.

Seated in his presence it felt as if time had come to a standstill, that all the rush imploded in the face of time, that man did not have in his power to force the cycles of Nature, like all other beings in the universe, man is most aligned when Nature speaks to him through him. I started to wonder if those thirteen intense days in the mountains were an illusion or did I really undertake that physical journey?

The hermit looked at me, and for the first time he smiled, for he saw upon my face my confusion. But I knew what he knew, that my journey through the mountains was real, for the essence of what the trip has awakened within me was doing its dance of joy in that space that transmuted through me; my hurting knee stood testimony to that fact. My journey through the mountains was not a journey towards a destination, rather the journey itself was the destination.

"Control the five senses which are hissing like serpents. The mind is jumping like a deer. Control the mind. Burn it in the fire of meditation. Strike it down with the trident of discrimination. You can attain me".

3. SHIVA – THE EMBODIMENT OF MATURE MASCULINITY

"I am the lord of delights and pain,
Of the pest that killeth, of fruitful joys;
I rule the currents of heart and vein;
A touch gives passion, a look destroys...
I am the God of the sensuous fire,
That moulds all nature in forms divine,
The symbols of Death and of man's desire."

(Alfred Lyall)

Believed to be born about 7000 years ago in India, Shiva lived in a time of confluence of two great races, the Aryans and the indigenous people of India. Spiritual scientists believe that He brought form to every facet of human existence, establishing ideals for the civilization of India, developing the foundation for prosperity, and giving purpose and direction to the masses. He is considered to have left behind the manuscript for humanity to live life in pursuit of oneness with the Cosmic Consciousness. Shiva is believed to have played a unique role in building human culture and civilization, sculpting a well-regulated social order, proffering principles governing marriage, family life and roles for man and woman, establishing codes of conduct for daily living and community spirit, developing the pathway for faith and spiritual development, consolidating the science of medicine, enriching music by stringing together the seven musical notes, creating a system for eating, education, upbringing of children, work ethics, sociology, institutional science and more of what was relevant to society.

Shiva is present in all walks of Indian life and is intimately woven into the fabric of Indian society. He is known as one whose personality had fully aligned with His principles, hence it is no surprise that He is seen as god in India. As much as Indian culture and civilization cannot stand without Shiva, Indian mythology cannot exist without Him.

* * * * * * * *

Mythology itself is timeless; it might centre on a real or a fictional person. It plays a big role in man's life, a role larger than rules, culture or collective social perceptions play. In fact, mythology has penetrated all of the above, and hence all aspects of humanity's existence. It is the product of humanity's collective unconscious over centuries and millennia. Generations of societies project their greatest aspirations and profound wisdom on to the mythological figure who then becomes a fountain of guidance for subsequent generations to tap into. Unlike with history, within mythology lies truth that is absolute to man, hence mythology is humanity's greatest wisdom-carrier.

Whether Shiva existed for real or not, He embodies the highest within man, and reminds man of the divine within him. This holds true for mythological figures of all ancient civilizations. Mythological figures from all ancient civilizations are fountains of wisdom for subsequent generations. Whether good or evil, these figures are archetypes of the various elements within man. They reflect back to him his grandest and his lowest, his noblest and his demonic. And in minds fertilized by curiosity, mythology turns into seeds of profound thought that enable man to discover his true personality, his *Svadharma*. The only word of caution is that he who applies the truths of mythology in his life must safeguard himself from the traps of dogma, he must use his *Viveka* (the power of discrimination) as the churning-rod to churn out the wisdom that brings mankind forward.

The mythological image of Shiva is the culmination of millennia of collective evolution of consciousness. What man has found divine about himself has found its place in the rendering of this image; the greatest aspirations that lie in the collective unconscious of humanity has been superimposed upon Him, the goodness and love that is inherent to all beings has been portrayed as His nature, the highest principles that have unified humanity have been projected upon the personality of Shiva. His image embodies the energy that permeates through all beings, He is seen as the field that holds and governs all beings.

The trident that Shiva carries with Him is the emblem of sovereignty. His drum represents the letter 'Om' from which it is believed all sounds of communication originated (7000 years ago, Shiva is the one known to have structured language and music). The crescent moon on His head indicates that He has mastered the mind perfectly. The flow of the river *Ganga* from His hair – as seen in some of his images - represents the nectar of immortality. Wearing the skin of the elephant denotes that He has controlled pride (elephant symbolizes the propensity of the mind, pride). His sitting on the tiger's skin indicates that He has conquered lust (tiger represents another propensity of the mind, lust). In some portrayals, He is seen holding a deer in one hand, which signifies His control over the tossing of the mind (the jumping of the deer denotes the tossing of the mind). His wearing of the serpent around the neck denotes wisdom and eternity. In the centre of the forehead, He has a third eye, the eye of wisdom. *Nandi*, the bull that is often seen sitting in front of Shiva represents the vital force of life. The *Linga* – the stone phallus worshipped as the idol of Shiva – represents *Advaita*, the oneness of everything there is.

In His divine form, Shiva is an embodiment of serenity and renunciation. He is considered the incarnation of the Cosmic Consciousness within which the world exists. He is the subject and the object, He is the experiencer and the experienced, He is the union of the inner and the outer within beings, the self and not-self, the ego and non-ego. Shiva is embraced as the god of consciousness, He is revered as the protector of his devotees, He is cherished as the destroyer of evil, He is worshipped as the god of beings and non-beings, He is known as the beginning and end of the universe, He is coveted as the individual soul's higher nature.

But in His primeval, primordial and physical form, He also represents the ultimate embodiment of the Mature Masculine. He is the benevolent family man to His consort and His sons. He is also the ascetic, free from desire and worldly attachments. He who man knows as Shiva is He who clothes himself with whatever comes by His way, who subsists upon whatever He gets, and who sleeps on whatever spot He finds. He lives His life in austerity and penance, seeking to develop greater self-realization, and hence liberate Himself from the bondages of His physical form. He is the teacher for those whose lives He has graced, serving in wisdom and love, and illuminating their paths towards self-realization.

Shiva carries within Him the duality found in all humans. In some tales, Shiva is known to have five faces, two on the right which represent virtues like love, care, protection and benevolence, and two on the left which represent the terrible within Him, that which is in man that subjects himself and others to misery and excruciating pain. The face in the centre plays the role of overseeing all the other faces. In His all-encompassing form, He also carries malignant forces, the dark side within man routine to all. As within Shiva, this demonic side is within man the antithesis of his inner divine, the duality which makes man complete in his human form.

The sacred river *Ganga* flowing out of Shiva's hair lock is a metaphor for the flow of life energies; it is the energy that brings love, purpose and unity to man, the flow of knowingness; it is this energy that brings the expression of acceptance to man, and through acceptance inner peace. The sacred river also stands for awareness streaming through beings, giving the blessing to the devoted to access the deepest wisdom of absolute truth. The sacred river stands for the flow of *Shakti* (the divine feminine energy) through Shiva. It is this flow of *Shakti* that brings passion to purpose, meaning to the mundane, fulfilment to the routine, and polarity to everything on earth. It is this omnipresent polarity that plays the symphony of cyclicality of all that is in the universe; the force that makes everything in the universe flow. This flow magnifies and manifests and becomes the essence of everything living on earth. This flow is part of Nature's intelligence. In the divine form of adornment of *Shakti*, Shiva is known as *Ardhnarishwara* (the half-woman God).

In this form, His right side is like that of Shiva, and His left side is like that of *Shakti*. One side has his own colour, the other side fair-complexioned; one side is covered with a tiger-skin, the other side with linen cloth; on one side there is a hooded snake, on the other matted locks of his consort's hair. In this manifestation, Shiva operates as the witness and offers the framework within which *Shakti* can manifest her fullest strength; he exalts the union of matter and energy, the Being and his *Shakti*. This portrayal of *Ardhnarishwara* represents the essence of the Mature Masculine.

He who man knows as *Ardhnarishwara* is He who personifies the unification of the masculine and feminine cores that resides within all men. Shiva shows himself as being all that is male, in harmony with all that is female within, through this form of being the inseparable unity. **Through the integration of His inner feminine, He represents the transformation of the adolescent masculine into the Mature Masculine;** in the process He has not feminized himself, He has simply elevated himself to the highest plane that man is able to achieve. When an uncut diamond is polished, its rough edges removed, it turns into a precious stone; likewise when the adolescent masculine integrates his inner feminine, he acquires the shine and glitter of the Mature Masculine.

4. LIBERATION: THE MATURE MASCULINE'S GREATEST PURSUIT

"Mana eva manushyanam karanam bandhamokshaya.
Bandhastu vishayasangi mukto nirvishayam tatha.
Na muktirtapana dhomatupava sashaterapi;
Brahmeva hamiti jinatva mukto bhavati dehabrit."[9]
[Mind is the cause of human bondage and liberation.
Bondage means attachment, and liberation means freedom from attachment.
Liberation is not attainable by penance, sacrificial rituals, and fasting;
Liberation is attained when one realizes "I am Cosmic Consciousness"]

It is the objective of the ancient texts to illuminate for man the concepts of the 'Pati' (Shiva), 'Pashu' (the bound souls), and 'Pasha' (bondage). 'Pati' (Shiva) is infinite and eternal, self-existent and self-contained, constant and indivisible, knowledge and bliss. 'Pashus' are the individual souls who are caught in the predicament of 'Samsara' (the cycle of life and death). Depending on the virtuosity or viciousness of these individual souls, they exhaust or accumulate the fruits of their 'Karma' (Karma being the bodily experiences of thought, word and deed). 'Pasha' is the web of bondage classified into 'Anavamala' (egoism), 'Karma' and 'Maya' (illusion or darkness or ignorance). These bondages come from the bounded soul's forgetfulness of the divine nature of its being, instead clinging on to the false notion of its finiteness. It erroneously identifies itself with the perishable body, and mistakes its body to be its true self.

Mastering its ego, cleansing its karmic repercussions, dispelling its ignorance, and rising up from the illusion of its bodily existence, ultimately 'Pashus' become one with 'Pati' (Shiva) through their meritorious life.

* * * * * * * *

It is the combination of the forces of *Shakti* (the divine feminine energy) and Shiva that drives the cyclicality of all that is in the universe. This combination of forces is the *Prana* (life force) that makes everything on earth flow. This perpetual cycle of **creation** and **liberation** is the process through which universe renews and self-perpetuates itself. This cycle is, in fact, Nature fulfilling its reason for existence.

Shakti is the force of creation. This divine feminine energy is the manifesting force that brings form to all. This essence of creation itself is not the purpose of the divine feminine. Creation, which is the process of bringing something into space and time, is but only a means of manifesting love; love being the pathway of turning the un-manifest into the manifest. The expression and experience of love is the greatest aspiration of the divine feminine, *Shakti*. In the manifestation of love, *Shakti* finds the fulfilment of her highest purpose.

Like when a picture is painted on a blank canvas, the picture is moved from the un-manifest to the manifest. This is the divine feminine force of creation exerting itself. From a field of infinite possibilities and unlimited imagination, through creation, form is sculpted by the divine feminine energy. This process is *Shakti* in action. This route from 'non-being' towards 'being' brings the experience of bliss to *Shakti*.

Liberation is all in man's mind, but it involves freeing himself from the bondages both in the physical and psychological realms. To be totally free, he must transcend the confines of his human reality wherein resides these bondages. When man transcends the limitations of his human body and his human mind, he starts to experience oneness with all there is. In that state of oneness, the Mature Masculine is not in conflict with anything external, because nothing is external to him. He experiences a sense of inclusiveness, an inclusiveness that goes beyond his family and beloved ones, to include all that is around him. In that inclusiveness lies bliss, bliss which has no relation to anything external to him. Shiva says, "In this state of oneness, shattering all bondages, they attain the supreme stance of eternal bliss".

Like when a painting is erased from a canvas, it moves from form to potentiality. The painting is freed from its confined form back into a colourful world of infinite possibilities, a world of unlimited imagination. This process of moving something from the realm of space and time to the beyond is Shiva in action. This route from 'being' towards 'non-being' brings the experience of bliss to Shiva.

The route from 'being' towards 'non-being' is the process of liberation. This process is one of constantly integrating man's inner duality comprising of the divine and demonic, the ego and the soul. Liberation is also the practice of aligning his personality with his philosophy; in other words, the act of identifying his life with his principles. Shiva's austerity and meditation is but His way of bringing awareness upon His duality, and transcending His demonic side. Similarly, the Mature Masculine chooses his path and practice that supports his purpose of reconciling his inner duality.

Entrapment of wealth, family, material pursuits, friendships, hobbies, social engagements, pursuits of power, position, prestige, success, ambitions, goals, etc. are examples of physical bondages. This is not meant to say that man must forego all the above. Rather the Mature Masculine asks himself what these mean in his life. He recognizes that he is not tied down by these pursuits, that his life is not consumed by his materialistic ideals, rather from a place of self mastery he experiences gratitude for what he has. From that place, he continues on his pursuit of expanding greater self-awareness and thus liberating himself.

The finite mind of man carries afflictions like complexes, inner conflicts, scepticism, anxiety, negative emotions like fear, shame, guilt, anger, etc. clamping him down in their vengeful psychological grip. To be trapped in the confines of the psyche is to not know the multi-dimensionality of every moment and its experience. Man's ego limits him through its need for identification. A man who is caught up in his ego clamours to belong, and to seek validation from those around him.

The consequence of being an adult is that mankind is pre-conditioned with self-enhancing ideologies and limiting beliefs, and these have often turned man into a prisoner of illusions. With these illusions go limited degrees of freedom in thought and expression. The Mature Masculine operates from the awareness that if left to his subconscious mind, he will remain an automatic actor of these pre-conditioned self-enhancing ideologies and limiting beliefs. Hence, he has liberated himself from the clutches of these ideologies and limiting beliefs by operating from his conscious mind, being in awareness during every thought, word or deed.

Another consequence of being an adult is that man has inherited expectations. Through a process of constant engraining that has spanned years of upbringing, the expectations that he has inherited from his parents, teachers and society in general have become his propeller in life. The Mature Masculine realizes that what is right for him – and for those he loves and for those in larger society and Nature - is already known to his most divine inner voice. Therefore, without judging if his inherited expectations are good or bad, he elevates himself above those expectations and uses his own divine inner voice as his beacon in life to propel himself towards lasting liberation.

The Mature Masculine has suspended his judgment, he has risen far above the range of his perceptions, and he has freed himself from the confinement of the experiences of the five senses. He recognizes that to judge is to take a position for or against something, hence qualifying something according to the preconditioning of his mind. Through the awareness that any shape, size or texture that he experiences is the result of his world view that he has acquired through his upbringing, the Mature Masculine remains free from the illusions of his mind.

Time is one of the whips that the ego uses to control man's existence. The unaware man gets caught up in the illusion that controlling his reality using time - which is an artificial construct of the ego – brings certainty and rhythm to life. However, this dependence on time only entraps him further to the ego through a physical bondage and resulting anxiety. Hence the Mature Masculine has transcended the trap of time, choosing to be led by his divine inner voice instead. He is aware that the guiding principle for his divine inner voice is the honour of all creations, and time and space plays no role in governing his actions.

At a karmic level, man carries memories that unconsciously govern his thoughts, words and deeds. Virtuous or vicious, these thoughts, words and deeds follow a continuous pattern of repeating and reinforcing cycles. The Mature Masculine chooses to disrupt these cycles of the mind by illuminating these cycles with his awareness and self-knowledge. Existing patterns are broken as he creates new patterns, this time governed by his soul. Memories – pleasant or unpleasant – have histories that go into his childhood or even past lives. Many memories carry with them actors from the past. While the Mature Masculine cherishes with gratitude the past actors involved with his pleasant memories, he rigorously forges ahead with his process of forgiving and letting go the actors involved with his traumas. His noble endeavour of feeling compassion for those perpetrators of his traumas helps him get beyond the anger he feels for those who have wronged him. All are the children of the Cosmic Consciousness, and in the experience of compassion lies merit. With meritorious act comes liberation from the bondage of the ego.

In closing, the prayer of the selfless Mature Masculine is as follows. Liberation is;

- A violence-free society
- A disease-free body
- A suppression-free heart
- A confusion-free mind
- An inhibition-free intellect
- Trauma-free memories, and
- A sorrow-free soul.

* * * * * * * *

In his daily practice of living his highest self, the Mature Masculine - who is on his path of liberation – asks himself the following questions;

- ✓ Knowing that liberation is all in my mind, what is my daily practice to liberate myself?
- ✓ Am I a victim of my worldly pursuits, or do I relate to my worldly pursuits from a place of self-mastery?
- ✓ How rigidly is my life governed by time? How do I balance my life rigidly lived out of my agenda, versus my life driven by the preferences of my heart?
- ✓ How is my adult conditioning constraining the free expression and experience of my child within?

5. FINDING WHOLENESS WITHIN HIMSELF

"Purnamadah purnamidam purnad purnamudachyaté;
Purnasya purnamadaya purnameva vashisyaté."
[This is whole, that is whole.
From the whole the whole has emerged.
If the whole is removed from the whole,
The whole remains.][9]
(Shiva Mantra)

It is said of 'Brahma' (the Cosmic Consciousness, whose reincarnation Shiva is known to be);
He is whole, unblemished and immeasurable. He is established in His wholeness – here, there, everywhere, in all directions, in all realms of existence and beyond. If from this Whole Entity is removed the whole Entity, what remains is still whole.

All entities have emerged out of that Whole; they are all being maintained in that Whole; and they will all finally dissolve in that Whole. He is the culmination point of all beings. He is the target of all life's urges, of all the inner vibrations of the mind, of all struggles of the heart.

Shiva brings about the unification of the transient with the transcendental, and of all that is illusory together with the ultimate truth. For new creation to take shape, that which already is, needs to be destroyed. Destruction must precede creation. Shiva plays the crucial role of destruction for creation - thus becoming both the creator and the destroyer. As the creator He becomes the symbol of mercy and love, while as the destroyer He becomes the icon of wisdom and renunciation. Also assimilating within Himself the characteristics of the male and the female, He represents wholeness - so elegantly captured in His depiction of the 'Ardhanarishwara' - the union of the male and female. Shiva is movement and tranquillity, light and darkness, and wild but compassionate. He is wholeness personified.

* * * * * * * *

It is the pursuit of the Mature Masculine to discover and live his wholeness. Wholeness for him is an undivided and unbroken completeness or totality with nothing wanting beyond that completeness.

By wholeness is not meant creating man's own private kingdom, raising walls and digging moats to preserve himself. He must realize that his wholeness shall never be accomplished through separateness, instead only through the oneness of existence in the Infinite. Try as hard as a frog may, sunlight can never be generated inside the kingdom of its pond.

Wholeness is achieved through the full integration of man's masculine and feminine selves. All humans possess the masculine and the feminine within them. For most men, the masculine is more pronounced than the feminine, as is vice versa for most women. This is Nature's design. Thus within each man resides all the faculties of both sexes that he is able to access and apply in life. The Mature Masculine is able to access his inner masculine and feminine attributes - without effeminizing himself – to bring wholeness to his life. You will see him ably apply masculine attributes like vision, purposefulness, intellect, etc. and feminine attributes like tenderness, caring, compassion, intuition, etc. in good measure.

The Mature Masculine recognizes that bliss has no external reference. As it says in the texts;
"Anandadhyeva khalvimani bhutani jayante,
anandena jatani jivanti,
anandam prayantyabhisam vichanti"
[From joy does spring all this creation,
By joy is it maintained, towards joy does it progress,
And into joy does it enter.]

It means that he being the creation of the Infinite, has not his source in any necessity. His joy comes from his fullness; it is his love that creates everything for him. It is his joy of the infinite in him that gives him his joy in himself. Thus the Mature Masculine does not rely on others or external objects to be the origin of his joy. Joy that find its origin in the external is transient and dependency-based. Whereas he does not rely on others to bring him the joy that he deserves as a son of the Infinite, with a wide open heart he receives with gratitude the gifts of joy conferred upon him by others. He does not turn away what is benevolently brought to him, he honours those presents as the Infinite's design.

This does not mean that man's individuality is his highest truth. On the contrary, there is that in him which is universal. If his existence were an island, and his life were an isolated beach of sand, and his own self was the only entity to consider, that would be cheating the design of the Divine. The Mature Masculine's greatest joy is in being the servant of the Divine, in recognizing the universality of all there is, and achieve more and more union with all beings, animate and inanimate. This he shall achieve from the place of wholeness.

Man can give from an inner place of scarcity, or he can give from an inner place of abundance. When man gives from scarcity, his action refutes the design of the Infinite. He has turned sadly into his incomplete self. His needs have overcome his reality, and fear has become his language. He is not perfect because his action is not free. There is incongruence between his intention and action. While such man's sight rests on his giving, his heart rests on what he seeks for himself in return. Man's bonding with those around him must be through his abundance in sharing. What else is a man's truth when he has all he needs, and is in union with all? The Mature Masculine's heart and sight are aligned and in symphony with his giving. He enthrals in the unlimited joy of sharing, and in that action he is living his Shiva within.

Man's state of 'being' is already complete, it belongs to his wholeness. That state is not attained from any necessity but from man's affinity with the Infinite, which is the perfection that he already possesses in his soul. Within him, he already has that where space and time ceases to exist, and where he is connected with all in unity. To 'be', is for the Mature Masculine to reside in that abode of wholeness.

The same holds for 'doing'. The 'doing' will not bring wholeness, unless it is an action that takes man to liberation. Such 'doing' then is not only existential but also spiritual. It is driven by the wish for the betterment of all beings. It transcends the limits of the present and the 'I', and falls on the side of the infinite. Man is securing his survival while purposefully moving on his path of Sadhana, spiritual practice. He is 'being' his greatest self in his 'doing', traversing towards oneness with the Cosmic Consciousness. This is the way of the Mature Masculine.

*　*　*　*　*　*　*　*

In his daily practice of living his highest self, the Mature Masculine - who seeks to find wholeness within himself – asks himself the following questions;

- ✓ Am I able to access and live with ease my inner masculine faculties (of vision, purpose, intellect, etc.), and my inner feminine faculties (of tenderness, compassion, intuition, etc.)?
- ✓ What is my practice of just 'being'?
- ✓ Is my every act of 'doing' aimed at my liberation?
- ✓ Am I able to give and take without experiencing separateness with the other?

6. HE IS IN ONENESS WITH ALL

"Anandadhyeva khalvimani bhutani jayanté.
Anandena jatani jivanti.
Anandam prayantyabhi samvishanti."[9]
[Out of bliss all beings are born,
in bliss they are living,
and into bliss they will ultimately dissolve.]

Shiva is oneness. His nature is 'Advaita' (indivisibility). The ashes that He adorns on His body symbolize the oneness to which all belong. It represents both the beginning and the end of all there is in the universe. Ashes are the product of fire, the energy of 'Prana' (life-force). This life-force is the origin of everything that begins from 'Brahma' - the Cosmic Consciousness - and manifests as beings, their instincts, sensorial urges, breathe, thoughts, speech and deeds. This Cosmic Consciousness is singular in nature and embodies life-force that is the sculptor of all there is. This life-force created Nature with its matter and its elements, which have taken life form.

Ashes also denote the impermanence of all there is. All life forms - having originated from the Cosmic Consciousness - are on their journey back towards oneness with the Cosmic Consciousness. Body perishes, form gives way for energy, and the ephemeral nature of living beings becomes evident. Intellect expands into intuition, and as a child rushing into the arms of its mother - intuition speeds towards oneness with the Absolute. As quickly as thoughts appear and disappear for man, do all the ephemeral beings in this universe appear and disappear for Him, Shiva. In the union of life and death is the union of oneness. To be illuminated is to recognize this truth of 'Tat Tvam Asi' (you are That).

*   *   *   *   *   *   *   *

The endless diversity visible to the limited vision of the human eye is deceptive. This diversity is but flashes of expressions on the face of the One, consciously designed to fool the un-awakened beings into cycles and cycles of *Karma* (actions leading to instant or future reactions). Through love and compassion, the Mature Masculine's sense of divisibility disappears, transcending the rigid boundaries of himself and reaching across the threshold towards the Infinite. Through love and compassion he recognizes that he is more than himself.

As is mentioned in the *Upanishads* (some of the ancient Indian texts);
"Na va are putrasya kamaya putrah priyo bhavati,
atmanastu kaMaya putrah priyo bhavati."
[It is not that one loves his son because he desires him,
but one loves his son because he desires his own soul].

It goes to mean that man finds his own soul in those he loves. The Cosmic Consciousness is in one and all. That's why the joys and sorrows of his beloved ones become his own joys and sorrows. This expression of his love for his family, children, friends, the Supreme and other beloved ones highlights the wonderment of oneness. It is in man's understanding of this unity that he is able to transcend his human fractiousness and be able to embody his highest self in all aspects of human life. Be it in his family or with teenage children, shifting his knowing to inclusiveness, in competition or business, shifting his knowing to collaboration, in civic life, shifting his knowing to compassion, in his daily interactions, shifting his knowing to understanding, the Mature Masculine lives by his higher nature, radiating his oneness, bolstering him to retreat from divisiveness seen around him.

However, when man sets limits to his love and compassion, he gets trapped in self-identification. His love becomes rigid and gets confined to his own kith and kin, he breeds selfishness, and he becomes insulated from the wider world and its beings. The originality of his expression fades away, and it gets replaced by a territorialism that makes him a brute. Neighbours cannot tolerate each other, nations are at war, battles rage among the sexes, parent and child get caught up in identity struggles, teachers who are meant to be the birth canal to enlightenment become impediments, societies are mired in over regulation, and mankind loses its authentic creative expression.

But that which seeks oneness in man sings;

"Asatoma sadgamaya,
tamasoma jyotirgamaya,
mrityorma amritamgamaya."
[From unreality lead me to the real,
from darkness to the light,
from death to immortality].

These are rites of passage to attain oneness. The Mature Masculine's joy lies in his assimilation of fear and love, pain and pleasure, 'being' and 'doing', creation and dissolution, manifestation and liberation. In his assimilation, egoism, *Karma* and *Maya* (illusion or darkness or ignorance) lose their expressions. He recognizes the illusory nature of the body, and the realness in him seeks for unity; unity in knowledge, unity in love, unity in purpose.

The practice of oneness for the Mature Masculine is also being in oneness with the moment, with the here-and-now, being completely oblivious of the past and the future, time and space. That is recognizing the divinity of the 'doing' that transpires at that moment, whether it is a job, an act of love, or a game. In his oneness, he is detached from outcomes of his 'doing', and his intentions are scripted to seek the welfare of himself and all. His oneness seems like playing in the symphony and being the conductor at the same time, melding together two opposites, being caught up in the act. Man and the moment becomes married in love, form vanishes in that union, and what is left is a cosmic pulp of oneness. In this oneness, the wave and the ocean are one, the mirror and its reflected image are one, ice and water are one, pot and clay are one. The *Atman* (individual soul) and the *Brahman* (Cosmic Soul) are in union, just like milk is inseparably mixed with water.

* * * * * * * *

In his daily practice of living his highest self, the Mature Masculine - who seeks to find oneness with all – asks himself;

- ✓ Am I able to open my heart and express my love and compassion for those beyond my kith and kin?
- ✓ Am I capable of viewing everything external to me as a natural extension of my very being?
- ✓ In my 'doing', can I become oblivious to time and space and create oneness between my 'being' and 'doing'?

7. HIS SOJOURN INTO HIS RESTFUL AWARENESS

"There is a shrine in the mountains
where towns-people go to worship and pray.
Very few ever take the trouble
to go to the inner shrine where our soul lives,
providing the spark of love that moves the world.

The soul's radiance is beyond words,
it is the source of all intuition,
it is the beauty of human existence,
it shapes all creative powers of the Universe
and it is bliss-personified." [35]

As 'Manish' (the conqueror of the mind), Shiva is the portrait of serenity and centeredness, sitting deep in meditation, the master of His mind and His other faculties. Shiva's sojourns into austerity and penance are His means to master His faculties and access His inner divine which is infinite in Its form and matter.

We notice Shiva as living His fullest karmic existence - His existence as a 'family man' being the guiding and protective father to His sons and as the caring man to His consort, Parvati. In His fullest non-karmic existence, Shiva is the austere ascetic being in meditation and restful contemplation. His example is an essay of seamless balance between active engagement (Pravritti) and silent withdrawal (Nivritti). In the fireside stories, His existence is a cosmic communion between the 'being' and the 'doing'.

* * * * * * * *

The context of man's modern life carries significant difference to the mythology of Shiva as heard in the stories handed down from generation to generation in its verbal form. Man today is trapped in the 'doing' world, the world where he is a task manager in his various roles as husband, son, father, employee, colleague, friend, neighbour. He is identified by what he does and what he has, and the association with his true self - his inner being - is forgotten. He dreams of a tomorrow where he can start 'being', away from the maddening crowd, away from his teen children, away from his tiresome job. Unlike a patchwork fabric, he has not weaved restful awareness and contemplation – his pathway to 'being' - into his 'doing' life in order to live his fullest potential. Man who lives in darkness will ever not persevere to open his full access to the Infinite. Therefore, his innate expression of discipline and self-restraint stays muted, and his personal purity of life remains a distant thought. As a result, the unlimited fountain of strength within him remains clogged, the influence that he has potential to wield remains corroded, his strength reveals itself not in beauty, his respect defies destiny to command.

Man has reason at his disposal, his *Viveka* (gift of discrimination) is acute, and he is equipped with conscious thought. He is born of higher consciousness than the beings of instinct, for he knows the distinction between virtue and vice, knowledge and illusion, good and evil. Beings of instinct have no such thing. But to tap into his highest nature, to tap into his greatest potential, man must reach into his deepest essence, lest he should sink lower than beings of instinct. This he can achieve. The Mature Masculine, through his practice of restful awareness and contemplation realizes the essential unity of the world with the conscious soul of man. Only he can live and express his inner divine of true ecstasy of joy.

Hence the saying of the *Upanishad* (some of the ancient Indian texts);
"Ekam rupam bahudha yah karoti tam atmastham ye anupachyanti dihrah, tesham sukham chachvatam netaresham"
[Only those of tranquil minds, and none else, can attain abiding joy, by realizing within their souls the Being who manifests one essence in a multiplicity of forms.]

Like a fish limited in its movement to either bank of the river, man's greatest destiny is confined to his pursuit of oneness with *Parama Purusha* (Cosmic Consciousness). However, as free as a fish is to swim upstream or downstream, man has the freedom to embark upon infinite pathways towards or away from his destiny. Through man's detachment from his 'doing', he can practice restful awareness of his intentions. What he wants to become – or un-become – he can by simply bringing his intention into his restful awareness, for intention is the thought that resides within the whole being of man, the vibration that percolates through every cell of his body, the sound that pervades every layer of the mind, the air from which the words flow like notes from a flute, and the source of all deeds. It is the propeller that ideates creation.

It is well said in the texts of the *Upanishads* (some of the ancient Indian texts);
"Sa yah samkalpam brahmety upasté kliptan vai sa lokan"
[He who meditates on will as *Brahman* (Cosmic Consciousness), he verily obtains the worlds he has willed.]

The more the Mature Masculine slips into the space of restful awareness and contemplation, the more he spawns his intention. Consequently, the more he empowers the forces of Nature to conspire towards his purest motive, and the faster he manifests his intention. His being becomes one with that intention, his reality merges with that intention. If man wants to become an athlete, the more he brings into his awareness his intention of becoming one, the more his physiology and psychology responds to reflect that intention. This is the power of restful awareness. He who sows the thoughts of divinity into his restful awareness becomes transformed into the divinity himself.

When man gets caught up in the flow of the worldly life of 'doing', he is tied up in his daily battle of solving his material problems. His loads are too much, life is unwieldy as simplicity evades him, his life is burdened with the mundane, and the greatest essence of the learnings from his past bear no benefit upon his present. To the fatalistic man, the future seems remote and beyond control. He is resigned as the future feels like a variable with dooming possibilities, rather than a wind to be harnessed upon the sail. He is devoid of purposefulness to attain oneness with the Absolute, or to unleash his might and live his divinity.

Upon modern man, it is well said in the *Upanishads* (some of the ancient Indian texts);
"Namo astu ayaté namo astu parayaté. Prane ha bhutam bhavyancha"
[That which is past is hidden in life, as it that which is to come.]

The highest masculine spirit is often in restful contemplation. In his restful contemplation, the Mature Masculine is able to access his infinite potential to connect the dots into the past and future. He is able to penetrate the grand conspiracy of the divine, the conspiracy that drives everything around him. In restful contemplation, he uses the gift of his intellect to connect the dots into the past, and taps into his intuition to connect the dots into the future. He recognizes that the past and future are part of a greater whole not separated in time. He realizes that he is an entity moving through a sequence of 'here-and-nows', each here-and-now an opportunity to manifest his most divine self and live his highest life purpose.

The Mature Masculine is he who can access all four states of the mind, viz. wakefulness, dream, deep sleep and *Turiya* (state of oneness with Cosmic Consciousness) at will.

It is said in the ancient texts;
"Jagrat swapna sushuptyadi chaitanyam yad prakashaté;
Tad Brahmahamiti jinatva sarvavandhé pramuchyaté."[9]
[The three states of wakefulness, dream and sleep are expressed by the Cosmic Consciousness; One who realizes that which is *Brahma* (Cosmic Consciousness), is liberated from all bondages.]

The wakefulness state is the state in which man is awake, and his conscious mind is in operation. It is the state in which the mind is in interaction with the material world, receiving input, assimilating and reacting to the external world. It is the state of physical manifestation, the state where man is in experience with the worldly reality of his gross body. His gross body is the one with its physical form, it experiences through its senses and expresses through its motor organs, it is material and destructible. The gross body is what he can see, what he can touch, what he can smell. This gross body, at any moment can fall ill, and at any moment can succumb to old age and death. Man – in his waking state - is caught in the midst of his sensorial experiences, and he attains his satisfaction by the varied enjoyment of his senses.

The dream state is when man is asleep but his mind remains active in thinking and recollecting. In this subconscious state, man is living the experience of his subtle body, a body subtler than his senses can perceive. This layer of himself is far from his sight, far from his touch, far from his smell. As in the waking state the gross body and the gross world seem real, so in the dream state the subtle body and the dream world seem real. In his dream state, man is unaware of his gender, and he experiences happiness and sorrow by the inner world created by *Maya*, his impressions, on the silver screen of the mind. His thoughts, memories, recollections and creative insights originate from this state.

The deep sleep state is when man is free from the bondages of the human body and the conscious mind. He has no thoughts in this state and possesses very limited 'I' awareness (there is some awareness, incomparable though to the awareness of the wakefulness state). All distinctions of the inner and the outer vanishes, there is no subject or object, no discrimination between self and not-self, ego and non-ego. His presence has elevated into the intuitive plane, and he is in experience of his causal body, the innermost subtle body that veils the true soul. The causal body is the body that endures over many incarnations, until man's self has dissolved into the Infinite spirit, and his causal body is the repository for all man's karmic impulses. In the state of dreamless sleep, man experiences the infinite and eternal bliss of his own presence.

The fourth transcendent state of *Turiya* is the background that underlies and transcends the previous three states of consciousness. It is referred to as *Atyanta-shunyata* (absolute emptiness in Sanskrit), the consciousness of the Shiva within. This state is a witnessing consciousness which is neither inwardly nor outwardly aware, nor with consciousness infolded upon itself; it is incomprehensible, without attributes, invisible, unimaginable and indefinable. Man – in this state of oneness - becomes all-knowing, as many spiritual scholars and masters of all times have demonstrated through the millennia. When man enters that realm of the mind, a realm where he is in connection with all there is, he has psychic experiences, he encounters departed souls, he foresees future events, and he becomes pure unlimited bliss. This experience is well captured in the *Upanishads* (some of the ancient Indian texts) as follows;
"Yad vava kam tad eva kham, yad eva kham tad eva kam iti"
[Joy, that is the same as ether; Ether, that is the same as joy.]

It is the ultimate end of the Mature Masculine to find the Absolute which is in him. Through restful awareness, the Mature Masculine accesses the three states of consciousness and beyond, so that he holds the key with which to manifest his fullest potential and harness all his faculties. His daily practice of restful awareness is to access the infinite potentiality of the Universe by becoming a channel to its powers, and sharpening his empathetic radar with which to tap into others' inner realities.

Mans' mind, which is the summation of his actions of his past and current lives – otherwise known as *Karma* – is limited by its conditioning. Through restful awareness, the Mature Masculine dissolves the residues of his actions, and when he has de-conditioned his mind, cleared it off all its *Samskaras* (the burden of consequences of his *Karma*), made it referenceless, then he attains the *Turiya* consciousness. Through his restful awareness, he endeavours to crack the code of the Divine conspiracy and own his ineffable joy, immeasurable peace and unity in love. Then the Mature Masculine finds in truth what he is.

* * * * * * * *

The Mature Masculine - who is a daily practitioner of restful awareness – asks himself the following questions;

- ✓ Have I compartmentalized my 'being' life from my 'doing' life, or have I woven them both into my life in harmonious balance?
- ✓ Am I able to slip into the space of restful awareness where the past and the future appear to me in sudden flashes of profound clarity?
- ✓ How can I consciously access that which is part of me, the subtle and causal layers, where I am the subject of unlimited and eternal bliss?

8. OWNING THE CHOICE-MAKER WITHIN

"Every journey has a beginning and an end.
It is the path that connects the starting point to the end point.
The path must provide the inspiration, stamina and direction
to enable us to reach the destination.
Herein, lies the efficacy and strength of the chosen path.

An ideal path brings happiness from the beginning to the end.
A mediocre path brings happiness either in the beginning,
or the middle or at the end.
A badly chosen path causes pain throughout the journey
and afterwards as well.

O' fellow travellers of this life journey,
Do not fear the path but understand it.
Avoid the roads that bring crevices of pain.
Choose carefully your diet, your thoughts, your actions, your friends,
and your objects of service.

Each step of the journey is a significant one.
Always take your steps consciously,
Fully aware of its implications,
Because a step away from the chosen path causes loss of time and
excruciating pain
and may sap essential vitality.

May the path you choose be a blessing.
Your path is important to you and all others as well.

Your pleasures and pains are the patterns of the cosmic-robe of the Universal Mind
and the beauty of your inner harmony provides a pleasant context for every entity in all of Creation."[35]

Desiring a son, Mrikandu undertook rigorous penance. A propitiated Shiva appeared before him and offered, "O Rishi, do you want a son who will live a long life lacking in virtues or a virtuous son who will live only for sixteen years?"

Mrikandu replied, "Let me have a virtuous son, my Lord". Soon after, a virtuous son named Markandeya was born to the Rishi. On the eve of Markandeya's sixteenth birthday, he found his grief-stricken parents in tears. As he became aware of his fate, he began to pray to Shiva with intense faith and devotion. At his preordained moment of death, as 'Yama' – the god of death – arrived and threw the noose of death around his neck, he embraced the 'Linga' – the phallic statue of worship of Shiva - and called out to Shiva for protection. Shiva appeared out of the Linga and forced the god of death to his knees.

* * * * * * * *

Man's every choice made today will carry with it its consequences into tomorrow. Known in the ancient Indian texts as *Samskaras*, these consequences becomes part of man's future, and reflects unconsciously upon his actions and decisions of the future. As a choice-maker, man holds within himself all potentialities to shape the next choice, and as a consequence, his own destiny.

In exercising his choices, he must remember with absolute certainty that essentially he is spirit. A preordained path is scripted for him, and he reserves the choice of progressing towards the Absolute or retreating on that path away from the Absolute. This he can do by developing mastery over himself, by rising above all pride and greed and fear, by knowing that worldly losses and physical death can take nothing away from the truth and the greatness of his soul.

Man is not a choice-maker because he can divide and conquer, but because he has the power of union. For centuries and millennia, man's quest to conquer and possess can only be seen as a victim hood to the traps of the ego. Being a weak being, he succumbed to the will of his ego while living the fallacy that he was a conqueror. Fortunately, alongside these stories of human weakness are also etched stories of men who have brought peoples together in a strong union of the heart. Though the stories of such eminent beings may not have received as glorious a review as their weaker counterparts, the Mature Masculine has risen and shone through all of history. It started 7000 years ago with Shiva, and continues over and over again until today. And it will continue until the end of time.

Similarly, the addicted pursuit of worldly delights is mistakenly recognized as mastered choice-making. In that pursuit, valuable resources are pillaged, man burns himself out, and precious time is squandered until he recognizes that the parade of illusory lights and colours has passed his doorstep. They have left no advancement in his life, except for some fleeting glimpses of satisfaction which have etched some memories lost now in time. What was his pursuit if not his victim hood to the screams of fear of the ego to urgently cater over and over again to its needs?

The conscious choice-maker chooses to live by his soul. Through the din of the countless voices vying for his attention, the Mature Masculine finds his own voice, the inner voice of his soul. He strains to listen to that gentle voice that whispers in dignity and poise, all-knowing through its energetic union with all beings, principle-centred in upholding the welfare of all, seeking to elevate each and every moment to greater heights of divinity through each thought, word and deed.

The Mature Masculine acknowledges the choice he has at every moment to embody the highest inner essence that remains covered within layers of his worldly being. In exercising that choice – whether it is through alignment with his principles, through active effort towards his purpose, through surrender to his devotion, through casting awareness and reinforcing his ideals within himself, or through other means – he becomes the mirror to those around to live their highest ideals. He does not exert control over those around him, he is undemanding, however his presence acts as a luminous beacon that affects awakening and transformation to the world around him. The Mature Masculine knows that he is the master of his inner reality, and that what is external to him is beyond his scope of force.

Every being around him – whether animate or inanimate - possesses its own mind however dormant or expressive that mind may be. So with all-round welfare in mind, the Mature Masculine sets intentions to leverage the Cosmic Mind and harness its immense manifesting power. Being part of the same continuum shaped by the Cosmic Mind, the Mature Masculine recognizes his choice-making ability to shape the intentions of the Cosmic Mind. All minds are integral to the Cosmic Mind. Hence through shaping the intentions of the Cosmic Mind, he shapes the state of each being through his pure, passionate and detached devotion to the Absolute.

As mentioned earlier, all-round welfare is a premise of intentioning. It takes self-responsibility to recognize that what is external to man is beyond the scope of his force, and he is entirely responsible for the reality he has created within or around himself. In the process of creation of man's reality, he has been endowed with infinite possibilities out of which he has chosen, either consciously or unconsciously, for a particular outcome. The house he lives in, the country where he resides, the chosen spouse, the friends in life, the values and belief systems he carries are all product of his conscious or unconscious choices. Every thought man has, every emotion he experiences, every sensation he feels are inter-related with his choices. Even when he has by birth surrendered to a faith or religion or cult or god, at the subtle level that surrender is propelled by his choice. Recognizing this universal law, the Mature Masculine refrains from presenting himself as a victim of circumstances.

We are all noble beings with noble missions destined for each of us. However, it is up to each man to choose whether to seek and embrace that service to himself and to other beings, or to subsist the existence of a generic cookie cutter. There is no condemnation on either, Nature is forgiving. The Mature Masculine puts the 'us' ahead of the 'I', not from a place of self-subjugation, nor from a place of victim hood, rather as a conscious choice-maker of his own life. From this place of self-mastery, his thoughts, words and deeds are accordingly tuned.

As firmly as he has suspended his judgment of others, has he insulated himself from letting the judgment of others be the guide in his life. For judgment can be a cruel thing. Like a blotting paper, it can impose upon man the darkness that resides within others. The darkness within all fails to see that the Self is neither beneath not above another, and it erroneously interprets humility to be weakness. As is elegantly presented in the *Upanishads* (some of the ancient Indian texts);
"Naham manye suvedeti no na vedeti vedacha."
[Think not that I know him well, or that I know him, or even that I know him not]

So what is the premise for man to judge? On the rare occasion when the Mature Masculine chooses to judge, he is keenly aware that within all beings – animate and inanimate - good and bad exists alongside, darkness and light exist side by side, but as a choice-maker he reserves the right to recognize and rejoice only the good in others. Like a snake shedding its old skin, in his journey to attain oneness with the Cosmic Consciousness, the Mature Masculine replaces his old *Samskaras* (the burden of consequences of one's good and bad actions) by suspending his negative judgments.

Buddha reminded us that all that man is, is the result of what he has thought before. Like ripples on still water, the impact of every thought travels from the realm of man's mind outwards into every realm of his being. Whether it is an impulse of the heart or impression of the mind, these ripples leave their impact in each part of the mind. Every voice of the mind has an echo in the physical body, for if not an echo of the mind, what else is man's physical body? At the grossest level, when man is possessed with anger or fear, his breathing and heartbeat instantly reflects those emotions. The trigger of his anger and fears reside in his thoughts. Unnoticeable to most among us, at the subtler level thoughts which generate the faintest emotion also have their echoes in the physical body. These echoes may be instantaneous or delayed. Or singular or cumulative. As the echoes of man's thoughts metastasize in the physical body, transformation occurs within. Being in the same field of consciousness, the ripples of the thoughts of every being travel in this field of consciousness to touch others, sometimes noticeably, often subtly. The Mature Masculine recognizes this and acts accordingly. As a choice-maker his thoughts are pure, his words benign, and his deeds life affirming.

* * * * * * * *

In his daily practice of living his highest self, the Mature Masculine – whose pursuit it is to own the choice-maker within him – asks himself the following questions;

- ✓ Knowing that everything external to me is beyond my control, how can I relate to external events with non-judgment, compassion and acceptance?
- ✓ Recognizing that I am a product of my choices, is my next choice elevating me further to my highest self?
- ✓ Do I feel like I am a victim of circumstances, or am I exercising my everpresent power of choice?

9. THE COMPASSIONATE OBSERVER ARCHETYPE

"As a shadow in the warm summer dusk
As a watchful falcon in the sky
As an observant swan mother in the water
Your omnipresence I feel

Over my thoughts and deeds
Guiding my intentions
Holding me gently by Thy hand
Lest I should trip and fall

Light over my darkness
Wisdom over my ignorance
Teaching me compassion
I am strong is Thy presence

Floating from unreal to real
Nodding Thy head in approval
Gliding from separateness to union
While feeling safe in Thy comforting embrace"

(Indian Folksong)

In this ancient tale, a group of Rishis lived as recluses, but were not ascetics: they had wives. As their penances and practice grew stronger, so did their ego. As they lost themselves in the pride of their powers, one day Shiva appeared in their habitat as an ash-strewn yogi together with

'Vishnu' (known in Indian mythology as the God of creation) who had transformed Himself into a heavenly maiden.

The Rishis were smitten by the voluptuous nymph, feasting their longing eyes with desire, thus throwing away the merits of years of hard penance and monastic life. The wives of these hermits rushed out at the sight of the yogi, driven by their lust, losing all their restraint. The hermits soon regained their senses and were outraged by the intrusion of the carnal apparitions into their lives.

As the wives poured out their frenzy in the form of their adoration, the hermits poured out their frenzy in another form, anger. In the presence of such raging forces, the centred yogi remained calm and serene in Himself. As the hermits threw their vilest curses and the weapons of their demonic inner archetypes at Him, Shiva – the supreme ascetic - remained unmoved and centred. As He stood over them in unlimited compassion, the Rishis and their wives soon awoke out their illusions and discovered the errors of their ways.

* * * * * * * *

The compassionate observer archetype of the Mature Masculine manifests through realizing the Mature Masculine's kinship with Nature, the creation of the Force of which he is part of. He realizes the essential unity of the soul of man with everything animate and inanimate. He has learned that the world is not merely what it appears to be to his senses, therefore he is cautious of the observations of his sensorial self; it being limited in its view, and its angle of perception too narrow to be able to gauge the inner essence of the universe. The Mature Masculine is aware of the ego's temptation for separateness, and he has deciphered that truth lies not in his power of possession but in his power of union. His archetype of compassionate observer awakens not through the power of winning – or being right – rather from the power of accepting and allowing from a place of choice. The compassionate observer does not flourish in an inner world of narrow necessities, rather in a world of exuberant sharing. He enthrals not in the annoyance of diversity and heterogeneity, rather in the sentiment of empathy for beings. He does not ceaselessly strain every nerve and muscle from his debilitating thirst for acquiring limited resources, rather he rejoices in expansive release in the truth of Nature's inexhaustible cycle of dissolution and renewal. He is not imprisoned in the limited pleasure of mere extravagance, rather he feels liberated in his eternal joy of sharing. In being so, the Mature Masculine finds himself in perfect truth, and in his truth his harmony with the All is established.

As a product of his own choices, he – and he alone - has shaped his destiny with his *karma* (past good or bad actions leading to one's current experiences of joy or sorrow). Action holds reaction; reaction that is by nature automatic, uncontrollable, dispassionate. Thus virtue brings its triumphs, and ill-thoughts, words and deeds bring their own pitfalls. Man is what he has made of himself, hence he may make himself what he wills. That if he has missed the right turn, he is not condemned to eternal darkness, and every moment is potent in the possibility of redemption and renewal. That he can shape himself in the mould of goodness through his good thoughts, words and deeds, or get caught in the egoistic trap of badness through vile acts.

The archetype of compassionate observer within the Mature Masculine recognizes that he does not experience his real self in his awakened state. That which is permanent about him, that which knows no pleasure and pain, that which knows no death and decomposition, that which is real is the awareness that he possesses in his unconscious state.

"Tad yatraitat saptah samastah samprasannah svapnam na vijanati"
[When a man is asleep, composed, serene, and knows no dream, that is the self.]

Thus says the *Upanishads* (some of the ancient Indian texts).

All his physical world of engagement is only a projection of his mental images on the silver screen of awareness. That his physical self is but a meagre extension of his mind, that his external reality is but a reflection of his inner reality, and through a simple thought, through a minute intention, he is capable of reshaping his physical reality. Every event in the physical world is a mere appearance and disappearance like waves on the ocean. To get to the real, he must get behind the forms of matter, the forms of physical life, the forms of mind. And when he has glimpsed the truth behind the forms, the Mature Masculine automatically, unconsciously becomes the compassionate observer. He does not get caught up in the illusion of his physiology or psychology.

In his harmony of truth, the Mature Masculine becomes the automatic witness of his external reality. He becomes equanimous to his external reality in the knowing that it is purely a fleeting experience of his sensorial human self. Hence he does not view the world as being a perpetrator, rather he sees it as the play of Nature, the *Lila* (divine game) of which the Mature Masculine is part of. Therein lays the compassionate observer.

Being the compassionate observer is not being indifferent to what is. On the contrary, it is being completely aware of all that is around while recognizing that what is external is but beyond the control of his limited reach and narrow field of the mind. The Mature Masculine is a compassionate witness of all his external relationships; illuminating his external relationships with awareness, and recognizing their transience. His awareness elevates him above the ego trap of unconsciously defining opposites; be it good and bad, positive and negative, enlightened and ignorant, light and dark. In his practice of non-judgment, he refrains from moral evaluations in order not to hinder the Nature's flow of divine energy.

As is the practice of non-judgment one side of the coin, so is man's victim hood to others' judgment its other side. It takes the supreme will of the Mature Masculine to remain the compassionate observer in the face of others judgment towards him, while refraining from being indifferent. The compassionate observer archetype sees another's judgment not as a perpetration, rather as that individual's self-victim hood to the trap of his or her own ego's inner pain. That awareness holds him back from jumping in the gutter with others writhing in their own pain. Being a reflection of Shiva, the Mature Masculine is endowed with the courage to keep it together in the face of pain, his or others. He is not indifferent, on the contrary he is sensitive and considerate in his presence and support, he is the sacred space for his beloved ones to get intimate with their pain, he is the shelter for those seeking to heal and un-limit themselves from the grip of their pain, he is the shade in the desert where others can access their infinite potential of the intellect, he is the empowering source where others can master their most precious inner and vast outer realities. He does this from a place of compassion, a place from which he helps others discover their path of liberation. Indifference - being the poison that contaminates the vast ocean of connectedness and intimacy – is not the mantle of the Mature Masculine.

In the very process of reasoning, man often loses sight of the destination. Reasoning becomes the end in itself, just another fleeting exhilaration of the softness of quicksand. Justifications draw him into a fencing match with others, and securing each square foot of the maze becomes the mission of his ego. Ultimately, his victory does not stand the test of time, nor does it measure up against the vastness of history and its deepest yearning for noble glory. Man becomes no more the compassionate observer, rather an insensitive victim of his inner pain in the moment. This is the nature of arguments.

If arguments are sparked by difference of perspectives, they are flamed by man's misplaced longing to win or be right. It is the process through which the individual wins as the collective loses. While the noblest purpose of an argument is to bring eventual oneness between two, often it metastasizes into a concrete barrier that leads to eventual separateness. Appreciation disappears, attraction for each other wanes, and any vestige of elegance or respect that remains for the man evaporates.

The Mature Masculine's compassion gives him the power and insight and beauty of mind to elevate himself above the limits set by his inner traumas. As the respectful observer, the Mature Masculine recognizes each individual's respective truths, accepts divergences, allows differences, nourishes individual equity, and lives his vows of self-honour and honouring other beings' truths. The indispensable nature of the compassionate observer archetype within the Mature Masculine shapes oneness between himself and other beings, oneness between himself and the Cosmic Consciousness, and his deeds take him to the highest peak and deepest reaches of his meaning. As the compassionate observer, the Mature Masculine's greatest gift is the gift of awareness to those in argument, his greatest role is the role of the propeller for inner shift, his greatest channel is the flow and overflow of the fullest within all beings, his greatest allowing is for the inviolable sanctity of every being, animate or inanimate.

*　*　*　*　*　*　*　*

In his daily practice of invoking the compassionate observer archetype within him, the Mature Masculine reflects on the following questions;

- ✓ Is my daily practice of detachment an indifference towards other beings, or is it being a compassionate witness?
- ✓ How can I let go of my ego's need to win against the other, to be proven right or to argue?
- ✓ Can I hold myself back from jumping in the gutter with others writhing in their own pain, instead being a compassionate observer?

10.MAN LIVING BEYOND APPEARANCES

"Anga Gaur Shira Ganga Bahayé
Mundamala Tan Chhara Lagayé
Vastra Khala Baghambar Sohain Chhavi
Ko Dekha Naga Muni Mohain"

[The holy Ganges flows from your matted hair. The saints and sages are attracted by Your splendid appearance. Around Your neck is a garland of skulls. White ash beautifies Your Divine form and clothing of lion's skin adorns Your body.]

(Indian Devotional Song)

The mythological story of Shiva and His consort Parvati's early courtship started as follows;
As a maiden, Parvati chose to serve Shiva in His practice of austerities, and as an ascetic He declined any necessity for a woman's service. Parvati countered, "The power of cognition (the masculine core) cannot exist without the force of manifestation (the feminine core). So why do You deny my presence?" Impressed by Her resolve, Shiva let Her serve His practice.

As the gods – out of their self-preserving intent - connived to create attraction in Shiva for Parvati, He resisted their attempts by immolating the god of love with His third eye, the eye of fire. Dejected by Her unrequited love, an inconsolable but resolute Parvati cast off the luxuries of Her parents, Her fine clothes and jewellery to spend a life of a hermit in the wilderness. She slept on the crude cold ground, barely ate a grain, and spent Her life in penance and thought of Shiva. After sustained devotion, She broke through His restraint and won His heart.

* * * * * * * *

External appearance is nothing but *Maya*, an illusion. This illusion is a deliberate creation of the Supreme Consciousness, since it reflects to man his own inner depth by exposing the value he attaches to external appearance. The artist is always present in his work as long as the work exists, similarly man's judgment will remain always in his experience of beauty. At the heart of his judgment lies his values, and beauty – for man – is the child of those values inherent to him. His level of consciousness is the barrier, and his values must wait for its elevation, for values are constructed upon consciousness. It takes a Mature Masculine to realize that like a blunt arrow failing to pierce an iron armour, lower consciousness fails to see beyond surface beauty.

The entire world is given to man, so why be trapped in the fleeting pleasure derived from the form? Man's relation to form is temporal in nature. Forms are perpetually transient, so their meaning to man changes with time. What is part of his truth today, what he is in relationship today with, is what brings meaning to him. When that form which brings him meaning today changes its aesthetic - for that is the unstoppable way of Nature - so does his relatedness to it, hence does his meaning derived from it changes. The transience of man's meaning from forms is an evergreen constant of the universe. That truth stands the test of time, it remains irrefutable. As the greatness of man is associated with his character, and not upon the radiance of his character, so does the beauty of any being depends upon its essence rather than its contours. Like the third eye of Shiva focused inwards at the mystery of his own being, so the Mature Masculine's endeavour to penetrate through the form of the world to its content.

The Mature Masculine has liberated himself from the diktat of social convention - which has defined beauty to serve its own unwieldy existence - to enjoy the beauty that his soul sees. Compliance to convention is the voice of the ego longing for social conformance. The ego's endless whispering of illusion has been borrowed from man's environment, to make him an instrument of the ego's yearning for safety in numbers. It strives to drug man with borrowed impressions, false in nature since what is true is what is within, lest man's authentic experience of beauty that originates from the soul be castigated by the egos of others. This the ego cannot stand. Out of its frightfulness, the ego urges man to adopt socially manufactured definitions of beauty lending to his higher feelings being suppressed. The ego flatters him into believing that he is free, and that he is sovereign in embracing others definition of beauty. It draws the veil over the eyes of his soul, and what is true for his soul is chained in a prison of misconception. His perception of beauty is fashioned by the mob-mind of his ego, and in his appreciation of beauty, in his rejoicing of creation, he is hindered by collective judgment.

This is not in the character of the Mature Masculine. His experience of beauty is connected to the unassuming nature of common objects, his experience of meaning is attached to the inner essence of all there is. He has not sacrificed his soul, he is unhindered by the restrictions imposed by his ego, he is full of the freedom of his soul's own experience of beauty. Thus he rejoices in the miracle of life.

"Indriyani hayan ahur vishayams tesu gocharan"
[The senses are the horses and the objects of the senses the path they range over.] So says the *Upanishads* (some of the ancient Indian texts).

When man's physical senses become his point of reference in life, beauty becomes the consort that pleasures his senses. Man loses his capacity to see things separate from the persistent urge of the lust of the senses, and his self-interest becomes his yardstick for defining beauty. His life mission devolves into self-gratification, and he becomes oblivious to the true expression of beauty that is everywhere. What is un-pleasurable becomes ugly, what is un-sensational becomes mundane, what fails to tickle his senses become untrue.

In the presence of the surge of his physical senses, his intuitional sense becomes blurred. He becomes incapacitated in connecting with that inner source within himself that is the ultimate illumination for the essential beauty of all there is. The path of liberation for the Mature Masculine bypasses his sensorial landmines, for only in that escape lies his connection to his intuitional sense. The neon lights of fantastic impressions, the flashy billboards of sensorial enticements, the passing parade of colourful experiences does not replace his celebration of the beauty of the core, rather it blends in harmony with the longing of his intuitional sense.

To forego the need to enhance man's outward appearance is to let go of the grip of his inner adolescence. It is to liberate himself from his need to be perceived in a certain way by the world around him. On the contrary, it is in his act of relinquishing his need to be perceived in a certain way that the

Mature Masculine radiates his magnetism to those around him. The Mature Masculine gives weight to his inner core, his own authentic expression, over any outwardly appearance needs that his ego may exert. It is said that Shiva finds all that he needs in his Self, needing not to bother wearing fancy clothes or cutting and combing his hair. This is the verse of guidance to the Mature Masculine.

The same ego that seeks and secures its appeasement also rapidly loses it appeasement when the novelty of the object of its desire disappears. This is true with objects and people. An attraction that the ego feels for the form of a person or an object wanes as quickly as it appeared. The Mature Masculine recognizes that everything external to him is an illusion. The experience of any external object is transient to the mind, and as quickly as the sensation comes it goes. The Mature Masculine recognizes that impressions can originate internally or externally and the mind cannot tell the difference between the internal or external triggers. The experience for the mind is exactly the same. Man can visualize the experience of driving a fancy car, and the experience will be the same or even far surpass the real experience of driving that car. This is the truth of illusions. The Mature Masculine's trick is to anchor his reality around his own inner essence, for it is the nature of the inner essence to seek and find its counterpart in every other being, animate or inanimate.

When beauty is not an inner idea which imparts joy to all man's activities and celebration to all his creations, when beauty is merely a value of external things, it is like the symphony to the ears of the deaf. The Mature Masculine recognizes that ugliness lies in the skewed perception of man, rather than in the elements of the Universe. The innocent inquisitiveness of the Mature Masculine's inner child opens up the wonderment towards the beauty of the essence of beings animate and inanimate, and through that innocent inquisitiveness he experiences his great harmony with Nature, and through that harmony he realizes his great spiritual unity with *Paramatman* (the Cosmic Soul).

* * * * * * * *

In his daily practice of transcending the superficial and living beyond appearances, the Mature Masculine asks himself the following questions;

- ✓ Of all that is close to me, am I connected closely to their forms or to their matter, to their appearance or to their essence?
- ✓ Are my definitions of beauty simple an inheritance of the social definitions of beauty, or are they my very own definitions?
- ✓ In my appreciation of beauty at this moment, am I being in honor of my physical sense or intuitional sense?

11.THE MATURE MASCULINE LOSING HIMSELF IN ECSTATIC ABANDON

"The grouping and regrouping of the constellations
The cyclical nature of seasons
The perpetual regeneration and renewal
This is the ecstatic abandon of Shiva."
(Unknown)

Shiva – in His form as 'Nataraja' (the lord of dance) - dances the 'Ananda Thandava' (a dance that depicts Him as the enjoyer of His creation) in supreme joy and creates, sustains and destroys with the rhythm of His dancing movements.

It is believed that the whole cosmic play is the dance of Shiva. All movements within the cosmos are His dance. The dance of Shiva represents the rhythm and movement of the world-spirit. All the spheres, the atoms and the electrons dance rhythmically. Atoms dance in the molecules and the molecules dance in all bodies. Seasons dance to the melody of time. Stars dance in the stage set by space. Various forms manifest and perish in Nature's dance of renewal. The dance of life moves to the drumbeat of Nature. The heart throbs its radiant shine of life, breath flows inwards and outwards in resplendent energy, blood flows back and forth in the constant flow of purgation and replenishment, millions of cells are in perpetual dissolution and regeneration, this is the dance of Shiva.

There are various kinds of dances attributed to Shiva. Many dances are an ecstatic celebration of the victory of good over bad, light over darkness, wisdom over ignorance, oneness over fracture, divine over demon. His dance is the celebration of the freeing of the soul from the clutches of illusion. He is in delirium after having done what He intends to do. In His steps and undulations, in His rhythmic dance, Shiva loses Himself in ecstatic abandon.

"Anandadhyeva khalvimani bhutani jayanté, anandena jatani jivanti, anandam prayantyabhisam vichanti"
[From joy does spring all this creation, by joy is it maintained, towards joy does it progress, and into joy does it enter], so it is said about Him.

* * * * * * * *

Ecstatic abandon is a place where reason shudders. Man's prim and pristine adult gives way to the playful child that has immersed itself into the intoxicating experience of the moment. The past and future disappears, and there is only the here-and-now. Day and night becomes non-existent, and it is replaced by the freshness and fragrance of dawn. The control and rigidity of the ego is replaced by the bliss and lightness of the soul. Ecstatic abandon unlocks the flow of laughter and frees the blocked energies that have got coagulated within man through the excessive work of the intellect.

Man has created an illusion of how he must conduct himself. As he progressed through generations, he has created a collective definition of what being 'adult-like' is. And he has learned to comply with that expectation, for social judgment is the punishment meted out to those who act out their inner child. To surrender into ecstatic abandon, man must free from the clutches of judgment, his own and those of others. The rigidity of the adult mind overwhelms man's capacity to surrender, and while he struggles to keep hold of his love by resisting his being's calling for ecstatic abandon, ironically in his surrender does man return to love.

The experience of the spirit is nothing but being in oneness. This is not a mighty and abstract rendering as seen propounded by numerous 'gurus' and spiritual seekers. It is neither an experience accessible to a select few who operate in 'other' dimensions. Instead it is an experience available to all, and even in the act of the daily mundane. Be it in the routines of cooking and gardening, or be it in the more esoteric practices of meditation or other rituals that take man into deeper or alternate realities, losing the experience of space and time, melding into the here and now, and experiencing the limitlessness of man's 'being' is the essence of being in oneness.

Ecstatic abandon is letting go of the masks that make man self-conscious and inhibit him in his fullest expression. Breaking through the ego, he experiences ecstatic abandon. The ego limits man to an intellectual interpretation of all that is around him, thus squeezing space for the intuitive and the experiential within him to present themselves to him. The ego is the root for the rigid concepts of the mind and all the preconditions and the patterns that drive man on autopilot in his daily existence of life. When man steps out of the basement of his subconscious space into the light of awareness, and when he operates using that light of awareness, he is free from the bondage of the ego, and he acquires the capacity to surrender into ecstatic abandon.

So is said in the *Upanishads* (some of the ancient Indian texts);
"Mameti badhyaté jantur nirmameti vimuchyaté"

[With the sense of mineness the soul is bound; with the absence of the sense of mineness it is liberated.]

The Mature Masculine loses his feeling of 'I', as when Shiva - in the icon of *Nataraja* (the lord of dance) - is dancing his *Thandava,* a vigorous dance that is the source of the cycle of creation, preservation and dissolution, and as when man is dancing to his favourite music away from other's eyes. He forgets his body and its reference to the surroundings. They are both merged into one, bound by love. As the Mature Masculine loses himself in ecstatic abandon, all his internal limits are overcome, and he has fallen into the habit of joy. He is no more naively bound in the misgivings of his ego. He recognizes that the descending road of the ego is only part of a whole which includes the ascending road of the soul. The finiteness of man's human existence may create artificial frontiers between beings, but the Mature Masculine has stepped up to being his true self, for in his true self resides his grandest experience of his soul.

Ecstatic abandon is man's surrender into the unknown. It is a matter of conscious choice, and the Mature Masculine has chosen ecstatic abandon into the unknown as his voyage to his joy and love in life. His surrender is a choice to be guided – rather than be forced - to his joy and love. The unknown is the vast space wherein lies infinite possibilities. The Mature Masculine is enchanted by this space where infinite possibilities for learning, evolution, renewal and transformation reside. As an adventurer, he leaps into this space, for therein lies truths about him. He is intent upon living the fullness of life and that includes facing his unknown. He is not dissuaded by the chaos that is the order of his journey, neither is he disturbed by the uncertainty that is the ticket to his surrender, rather he sees in his ecstatic abandon the opportunity to reshape himself into his fullest at that moment.

The Mature Masculine releases life from the bondage of fear and he unlocks himself from the grip of his ego, when he lets the moment guide him. In letting the moment guide him, in emulating the dance of Shiva as *Nataraja* (the Lord of dance), his mission is not forgotten to him. On the contrary, his mission is deeply embedded into his subconscious, and it reverberates within every cell in his body. In his ecstatic abandon, he is in unity with the Cosmos, and his mission is in alignment with the transforming force of Nature, hence his mission becomes the tune to which the Mature Masculine dances in ecstatic abandon. In his surrender, his mission guides him from note to note, from beat to beat, until the whole beauty of the song unravels in front of him and the full joy of the composition courses through his being. His devotion to the way of the Infinite is the source of his exultation, for on the way will he meet his destination. Devotion is the expression of the heart, the experience of the soul. Devotion begins where the rational mind ends. As such it is indefinable, but its experience is real. It is unifying because it always seeks and finds itself in others.

Through the act of life and past lives, man has ceaselessly accumulated impressions upon impressions in his being. These impressions have coagulated into his thoughts, his values, his physiology, his psychology, and most relevantly his traumas. Like the reins in the hands of the charioteer controlling the horses, man's traumas have a grip upon all faculties of life, his physiology, his psychology, his propensities, his thoughts, his words, his deeds. Unknown to man, his traumas have found a holy place deep within him to lead his life from, and he finds himself the silent witness of his thoughts, words and deeds. He is perplexed with his lack of control of his faculties, and that lack of control further dissuades him from plunging into surrender, into ecstatic abandon.

It is said in the *Upanishads* (some of the ancient Indian texts);
"Tayoh shreya adadanasya sadhu bhavati, hiyaté rithad ya u preyo vrinité"
[It is well for he who takes hold of the good; but he who chooses the pleasant fails in his aim.]

Man remains cold and distant to his traumas, building high walls between himself and his traumas, the curtains fully drawn so that the deafening sound of his traumas do not violate his sanity. Man mistakenly believes that his traumas are better left untouched, and the farthest he is from the arms of his traumas, the most out of reach he is from his traumas, the better he is able to operate out of his mastered awareness.

Like bubbles that rise from underwater, the Mature Masculine's ecstatic abandon into life unlocks the energetic bubbles of his traumas from the deep recesses of his subconscious. He does not go around it, for he knows that he cannot stand outside his traumas and invoke healing. In his surrender, long forgotten memories resurface and traumas harboured within reawaken, making him fully aware of them. In his intimacy with his traumas, his heart's suffering becomes visible to him, and the healing of his pain begins in his community of his whole. He creates a sacred space for his pain to rear its head, and like a sleeping serpent unfurling its head to the tune of the snake-charmer, his compassion becomes the wand that guides his pain to its dissolution. He enters in surrender into his traumas, and remains in persistent oneness with it. In his intimate embrace of the actors of his sufferings, his pain transmutes into forgiveness, and he reaches the void of lightness and peace.

In ecstatic abandon man becomes oblivious of his bodily existence. His sensorial experience is replaced by the ecstasy of the soul, and he finds himself enveloped by the naturalness of his true being. He is in exultative oneness with the force of Creation, and love becomes the element of his being. Love is incomplete until man has surrendered into life with his fullest passion and ecstatic abandon. Like a raft being carried to its destination by flowing water, surrender into life takes man towards his assigned higher purpose. Hence it is the highest passionate intention of the Mature Masculine to own his freedom from self-conscious effort. Freedom and true love exist in relatedness to each other, not as opposing forces that need to be brought under man's sway, rather as ingredients of perfect relationship. The unbelievers have proclaimed that freedom is the flight of man from love, love that is the very essence of his being.

It takes a mature masculine to acknowledge the inseparable existence of freedom and love, as inseparable as two sides of the same coin are. In freedom, love becomes unconditional, and it becomes part of the Mature Masculine's element of 'being' while ceasing to remain an act of his 'doing'. Love comes to him when he stops forcing it, it appears in his life when he desists from pursuing it. Like the bliss experience of the absorbed devotee, like the indefinable lightness of the meditating, like the artist losing himself in the rhythm of the dance, through choice the Mature Masculine slips into the oblivion of ecstatic abandon, the place where he experiences his delirium. In his love, he has transcended the narrow reality of his physical existence, where time and space acquires remote meaning.

* * * * * * * *

In his constant surrender into ecstatic abandon, the Mature Masculine reflects daily on the following questions;

- ✓ Am I able to free myself from the established social rules and norms of how I am expected to conduct myself as an adult?
- ✓ Do I feel free from social judgment when I express my inner child?
- ✓ How courageous am I in healing myself by surrendering into the dark recesses of my mind and connecting with my traumas?
- ✓ Do I let go and let love happen, or do I remain self–conscious and force love to appear?

12.SYSTEMATIZING TO GET TO THE TRUTH

"Ma go amar ei bhavana
Ami kothay chilam, kathay elam
Kothay jaba nai thikana."[9]
[Oh Mother, this is the only thought in my mind:
Where was I? Where am I now?
Where shall I go? I know nothing about these matters.]
(Bengali Passage)

Society is a system composed of many parts which are in relatedness with each other. Systems, protocols and networks govern society, and collective resources and objectives lend into society's reason for existence. Before Shiva, a well-regulated social order was not yet evolved. Social life was not at all systematized. It is believed that Shiva played a unique role in building human culture and civilization, hence Indian culture and civilization cannot stand without Him.

Among the principles that govern mankind as we know it today, the principle governing family was one of them. Shiva proposed that those who choose to bear off springs should also take up the responsibilities that go with it. While men took on the role of the protector, women became the nurturers for the family. Those who choose for single hood should embrace celibacy, simply because that ensured freedom from family responsibilities, freedom that could be channelled into exploring higher meaning that can benefit society.

Shiva instituted the principle of marriage. He assigned a specific role for the husband and wife, a role that lend to the most benefit for man, woman and child. Once the man and woman consented to these roles, they were considered married. With the institution of marriage, men started to take household responsibilities. Those who were previously devoid of social consciousness, they started to give form to communities, filled with inclusiveness and bonding.

Shiva established codes of conduct for daily living. These codes of conduct were meant to bring the greatest fulfilment in the material, intellectual and spiritual spheres of life. He identified practices that would support individuals in the pursuit of their happiness.

Shiva strengthened the foundation of mankind's mutual relationship by creating greater awareness towards the advantages of living in communities. With walls come animosity, with animosity comes vendettas, with vendetta comes destruction. Destruction means that mankind was constantly consumed with its quest for survival. Recognizing this, Shiva brought down the artificial walls of separation between the clans. He made it possible for all to meet and eat together as one big family.

Shiva developed the pathway of worship and spiritual development, and taught mankind how to evolve their psychic and spiritual selves through the various faculties of yoga (mantra, meditation, physical, energetic, intellectual, etc.). ´Tantra´ is known to have existed before Him, but He gave a systematic form to it. He created alignment between the scattered ´Tantras´ and each individual's urge for their highest fulfilment.

Before Shiva, the science of medicine was nothing but a disjointed assortment of substances that had healing properties. The medicinal value of these substances had been discovered accidentally. He compiled a science of medicine to save mankind from the scourge of diseases.

Based on the sound of seven creatures, Shiva is believed to have developed the seven musical notes. Even to this day, all music is based on these notes. Rhythm became delightful. That was not all. Based on phonetics, He developed 'Mudras', subtle gestures of the limbs and body that led to the synchronizing between music and dance.

Further, Shiva created a system for eating, education, upbringing of children, work ethics, sociology, institutional science and more of what was relevant to society. He structured the answer to humanity's perennial questions; Who am I? Why am I here? What is this universe? What is God? How is Nature governed?

All the above were expressions of Shiva's systematizing gift.

* * * * * * * *

Man is in constant endeavour to find balance in his physical, psychic and spiritual lives. Balance he achieves by using his reasoning to control the unknowns and the uncertainties that are resident beyond every new frontier. And when man has deduced the reason behind the balance he has created in his life, he explores the limits of his balance to find a new equilibrium in a greater plane in life, for it is in his nature to do so. This upward cycle continues forever, until the Mature Masculine has mastered all the limitation of his narrow human self, and he has liberated himself to become one with the Infinite.

Man's longing for limitlessness drives his endless synthesis, for when he has set himself free from the narrow limits of his material and psychic existences, he is immersed in the bliss of being enjoined in unity. His synthesis is but his search for the truth that governs all in the universe, the truth that encompasses facts, the truth that unlocks the bondages of his life.

This propensity is well encouraged in the texts;
"Satyam tva eva vijijnasitavyam iti"
[But one must desire to understand the truth.]

Wood burns to ash, wax melts, water evaporates into steam, man can endlessly collect facts, but when he learns that anything that is subjected to fire will burn, he can dispense with disparate facts bound together by a common truth. This process of synthesizing facts to discover its underlying truth takes the Mature Masculine beyond the frontiers of his limited human existence to the plane of bliss.

"When man knows a single particle of clay, he knows all objects of clay. When man knows a single grain of gold, he knows all objects of gold," so is stated in the Upanishads. When man has connected the reason of the mind with the play of Nature, in his knowing he can finally surrender in devotion to his daily practice of self-realization. This is the systematizing trait of the Mature Masculine.

Chaos is the nature of engagement. In seeking the union of his self with the Cosmic Soul, the Mature Masculine nurtures engagement, not shying away from it for fear of chaos, for chaos is inherent in engagement. Chaos gives birth to meaning, and it is the endeavour of the Mature Masculine to channel chaos into meaning, and bring reason to emotion.

It is also the imperative of the Mature Masculine to bring out the most authentic expression of each individual that touches his life. He is not swayed by the differences, he is not discouraged by the divergences, rather he is inspired by the infinite possibilities that lay ahead of him as he aspires to shape convergence, cultivate allowance, and practice acceptance, for therein lies the gem of truth that propels him forward towards his highest pursuit. This is the systematizing power that resides within the mature masculine.

The truth is already known. Lying among the debris of impressions, thoughts and vibrations that constitute this universe, every truth, every invention that is relevant to man already resides hidden. Teachers have graced this planet and left, leaving always the feeling among men that their departures have been premature. Nothing is farther from the truth.

"Yada vabhavyamasti"[9]
[whatever will be, will be.]
So it says about the perfection of Creation. Man must realize that the presence of every true teacher is pre-ordained, as preordained as his very own presence on the planet is. Teachers have come and gone, but the teachings have remained, for every teacher is but a mere messenger of truth, a mere courier of wisdom. Having delivered their task, having fulfilled their reason to visit, they have - by conscious choice - released themselves from their physical existence. Their arrivals have never been too late, neither have their departures been too early. Their messages have never been incomplete, nor have they been in excess. For the time man lives in, and for the consciousness he possesses in that slice of time, the truth relevant to his shift in consciousness has been presented to him, for it is the nature of the Absolute to bestow every resource man needs to attain oneness with *Parama Purusha* (Cosmic Consciousness).

This knowing powers the Mature Masculine to sift through the debris of impressions, thoughts and vibrations that constitute this universe, and uncover the truth. He aspires to crystallize its form, systematize its essence, and shine light upon It so that it becomes comprehensible to the simple minds, so that all beings can step out of the well of darkness, for that is our collective longing. It is the Mature Masculine's mission of every moment to live by the truth that furthers him in the cycle of consciousness.

Man who knows Nature knows its design for plants to blossom in Spring. To the Mature Masculine, systematizing means to identify this relationship between the universe and its beings, and to deepen understanding of the forces that govern these relationships. His joy comes from the manifestation of his innate gift of systematizing, for in its application he fulfils his noble intention of leaving the imprint of his legacy in the hearts of later generations. For 7000 years, starting with Shiva, the Mature Masculine has served humanity in his systematizing avatar, by bringing the truth of Nature close to us, by bringing the unknown into man's comfort zone, by bringing the adventure into the foreign, by bringing the divine into the profane, by bringing understanding into man's darkness, by bringing the future and past into the present, by bringing awareness into choice-making, by bringing knowingness into man's actions and reactions, by bringing energy into the heart's intuition for welfare, by bringing the infinite organizing power of the mind to our disposal, and most significantly, by bringing union between man and the Infinite.

* * * * * * * *

In applying his gift of systematizing in order to get to the truth, the Mature Masculine always asks himself;

- ✓ Am I inquistive about the truth behind the facts?
- ✓ Does the unknown and the uncertainties of new environments and new encounters discourage me or excite me?
- ✓ Do I often enough stop myself to ask why (for everything that is happening around me)?

13.GENTLE IN MANNER, RESOLUTE IN DEED

"Like an arrow from His bow,
Piercing the air,
Heading for its destination,
Oblivious to all that is around,

The trickling of the sparkling stream,
The wondrous colours of the unfurled feathers of the peacock,
The vibrant sounds of the early birds
The intoxicating fragrance of the spring flowers

The Cosmic Mind is resolute
Unwavering in its pursuit of the divine
For one and all
To come back to Itself

Filled with benevolence,
Exuding warmth and tenderness,
It takes us all in love on to Its lap
Seeking to bring us to the realm of eternal joy."

(Unknown)

A mythological story indicates the origin of Shiva as ´Ardhanarishwara´ - where He is depicted as half-male and half-female - the union of substance and energy, the composite of Being and His Shakti (force). The right half - depicting the male - is His own form and the left half - depicting the female part - is His consort Parvati. This depiction represents Shiva as 'Sadashiva' - the primeval Being - as being the unity of existence. It underlines the fact that division in Nature between male and female, between material and energy is only superfluous and in reality all is one. Shiva shows Himself as being all that is male and all that is female - through this form of being the inseparable unity. While the masculine in 'Ardhanarishwara' is the expression of determination, boldness and resolve, the feminine in Him is the embodiment of affection, tenderness and love.

This passage says it all. In His endeavour of sculpting the foundation of society, Shiva was not swayed by the discouraging forces that surrounded Him. His conviction was the ox, and His mission was the cart. He was led by His principles, and the all-knowing that He was, He saw the legacy that He would leave behind. But His resolve did not make Him incognizant towards the sensitivities of those beloved to Him. The mythological stories narrate Him as one who was affectionate and gentle towards His beloved ones. In His conduct towards those around Him, in His dealings with people, He was known to be tender and soft-hearted.

In order to align His life with His purpose, He used the power of his intellect, persistence and persuasion. And His magnanimity appeared when those around Him saw His wisdom and path, easily and instantly forgiving and embracing them unto Himself.

* * * * * * * *

Resolve is not, in the Mature Masculine, merely an ornamental quality; it is immanent, part of his fabric itself. He is resolute, because he is a mature masculine. His conviction of his principle is so firm, his feet so concretely planted, that sometimes humanity stands in real trouble before this immensity which unfolds itself before humanity, across all time and space. The Mature Masculine, more advanced in the path of virtue, succeeds - sometimes at the cost of inner and external conflicts of which he alone knows the hardship - in mastering the propensities of the mind that deflect him from his real goal.

Of this inner conflict, is said in the ancient texts;
"Yada vai nististhati, atha shraddadhati, na nististhan shraddadhati nististhan eva shraddadhati"
[When one has resolve, then one has faith. One who has not resolve, does not have faith.]

Humanity measures how great, under certain circumstances, is the responsibility of the Mature Masculine, for that responsibility is self-erected. No outside agent is the benefactor of that responsibility, for if responsibility must be thrust upon him, he is not a mature masculine. His belief is his beacon, his conviction is his god, the spirit that drives him towards the greater good, towards his giving, towards his meaning, towards his fulfilment and joy, for none else knows him any better than himself. His resolve finds its origin in his faith, his faith not in something beyond his comprehension, some abstract entity that is indefinable and remote from his inner essence, some distant or dogmatic notion that is not communicable to his fellow beings, rather faith upon that Self that is the voice within him. Such is the truth of the resolute Mature Masculine.

With resolve, the Mature Masculine pursues his highest purpose, and momentary distractions get not in his way. He does, while on his mission, surrender into the moment and taste the elixir of the here-and-now, for like a loose pet that comes home for its refill of water before continuing its gaming, the elixir is his stopover before surging further on his path. As the actor in the play of his life, the Mature Masculine is in oneness with the present, melding into the love that makes each moment, drinking his fill from the jar of joy that is the present. As the spectator of the play of his life, he carries in his mental armoury a flashlight that is ever shining its light upon that purpose that is the reason for his existence. The flashlight loses not its luminosity, for it is powered by his indefatigable resolve.

Man's ability to face disappointments - his and others' - is his power of staying the truth and living his mature masculine self, for that which is divine within him, his inner source, is an inexhaustible force for whose sake saying good bye, or rejecting an offer, or saying no, means little. For, every encounter is but humanity's test of his infiniteness, which is the true nature that is constant within him, there being no hint of battle nor self-serving desire for victory in its tests. Humanity honours, albeit unconsciously sometimes, that the Mature Masculine's 'no' towards it is a 'yes' for the voice speaking from his Soul, for Its very presence is to ascertain the Mature Masculine's resolve to nourish humanity's welfare.

Man who is steeped in ignorance about the fundamental nature of gentleness is inclined to interpret gentleness as weakness, or to label it as self-debasing or belittling of himself. The very thought that gentleness is the expression of his self-love – for he who loves not himself cannot mirror that experience upon others – which at once ennobles him and snaps his chains. To err is human, that man is fallible, for what is to be said of he who is in constant effort against Nature and its progenies to secure his material means. Gentleness, when its origin is in the compassionate heart of the resolute man, can be the soothing force and catalysing agent for the erring to find their light, and the fallible to find their courage.

The resolute man recognizes that gentleness does not negate his masculinity, nor does it subtract relationships, rather it adds to the resource of love and understanding. To the resolute man who finds his centre in his soul, gentleness becomes the energy that harmonizes all warring elements and unifies those that are apart, that it reduces all humanity's isolated impulses and impressions into fruition in love, that all the infinite details in man's life get bound in togetherness, and all humanity's thoughts, words, deeds and reaction unite themselves inseparably in peace. In gentleness, that which is One within the Mature Masculine is ever seeking for unity.

It is the deep resolve that comes out of the profound knowing of the Mature Masculine's *Dharma* (purpose of being) that makes him gentle, for the man who is anchored in his *Dharma* is unshakeable. He is not threatened by happenstances around him, he is seldom rattled by the twists and turns of his path upwards, he feels not that his mission is threatened by dark forces, thus he remains centred. On whatever step he resolves, whatever action he attempts, his solidarity towards his *Dharma* unites his resolve and his actions with the Infinite. When man is anchored in this union, and when this union is sculpted in cement, he is open to express his gentleness, which is his true nature, for his gentleness does not deviate him from his path.

How far man is gentle in his expressions, thus far communication is in its expression, for it is man's soul that draws others out of the shelter of their private impressions and interpretations. The Mature Masculine will ever persevere to keep communication undefiled, welcoming the other to shed his barriers, engage with open heart, and be himself rather than perform to another's script. Resolute, man may be about his mission, and earnest he may feel for others, he however is also the choice-maker for the colour of the ink in which communication with him is scripted; whether the hue of fear creates an impediment to the open exchange of thoughts and preferences, or the richness of love catalyses it.

Gentleness is the lubricant for communication, for then communication becomes free from the impurities of suspicion, animosity and anger, and lets trust grow stronger. With the disappearance of abruptness, humanity can serve itself better, disconnect and discord becomes fewer, and occasions of understanding flow faster. The earnest Mature Masculine, who, reconciling the firmness of his purpose with the gentleness of his demeanour, is able to reap the fruits of his open heart straightaway.

Man's human form is a product of his nature and nurture. The nature of his human form is what he is born with, it being his genetic expression at birth, which expression includes all that he has inherited from his parentage. Science today seems to converge with the ancient wisdom that man is not a static entity born for the first time in this birth, but he is a being that has travelled through various lifetimes, and this lifetime is but just another birth event in a string of births. Mankind's collective rational mind has started to accept this fact, and with this acceptance comes the added understanding that in this continuum of lives, man also carry with him experiences and memories – otherwise called *Samskaras* (the burden of consequences of one's good and bad actions) – from his past lives.

This nature, that is human in its composition, is adulterated and swayed by the propensities of the ego, and may exhibit vanity, mine-ness mentality, anxiety, envy, fear, indulgence, yearning for possessions, argumentativeness or repulsive expressions, any of which belittles rather than cherish others, expresses in unrefined ways rather than act in gentleness. Underlying this nature that is human, and thus transient, is man's absolute nature, the nature that transcends his human self, that nature which is incomprehensible, without attributes, invisible, unimaginable and indefinable. Gentleness is part of this absolute nature of man. There is no other expression so truly man's own, one that conditions a universal system of bonds and undefined relations in humanity.

In the ancient texts, it is said of Shiva's true nature;
"Kriya-gunair atma-gunais cha tesam samyoga-helur aparo pi drishtah"
[Having Himself caused His union with His duality, through the qualities of His acts and through the qualities of His body, He is seen as another (unified).]

Shiva knew His values, He lived by His principles, and He applied His values and principles as the framework of His life. This framework served Him as the fence within which He was gentle, open and receptive to the views of the other. Resolute as He was, Shiva married in oneness views of His with those of the other, through gentleness built union of perspectives, that of His and that of the other, through care created space for synergies of thoughts, that of His and that of the other. Within the fence of His *Dharma* – and only within it – He drew from His gentleness, full of compassion and understanding, full of acceptance and allowing, firm but gentle in His knowing.

The Mature Masculine looks down not upon others from the insolent height of his knowing, instead he humbly recognizes that what to him is a non-issue may be to the other a burning matter. He therefore treats the other with the utmost gentleness and love, and keeps his confidence in his own purity to transmute the other's concern into energy of the highest type. He therefore becomes the other's authentic friend, giving the other his fullest confidence, and with inexhaustible patience, gently explains to the other the moral basis of his position and action, the driver behind his principles and the pillars of his solidarity. In the process, many things within himself that were not part of his awareness before become clearer, and his self-realization elevates itself through his daily practice of gentleness.

* * * * * * * *

In his daily practice of integrating his resolve with his innate gentleness, and living his fullest self, he asks himself;

- ✓ To what extent do I reconcile the sight of my purpose with the joy of the present moment?
- ✓ Am I in self-honor of my innervoice while living in honor of the voices around me?
- ✓ Is my communication with the other motivated by my fears or my love?
- ✓ How aware am I of my vision and principles, their impact upon the other, and are all my daily actions aligned with my vision and principles?

14.AUTHENTICITY - HIS GREATEST EXPRESSION

"Till you've earned
knowledge of good and evil
it is
lust's body
site of rage
ambush of greed,
house of passion
fence of pride
mask of envy.
Till you know and lose this knowing
you've no way of knowing
my Lord white as jasmine."
(Mahadeviyakka, South Indian poetess)

It is told in the ´Puranas´ (the ancient Indian narratives of the history of the universe and the gods) that Sati, Shiva's consort, entered the flames in protest of Her father Daksha's dishonour of Shiva.

Shiva, in fury and anguish, carried the body of Sati and began to perform ´Rudra Thandava´, the dance of destruction, and wiped out the kingdom of Daksha. He became one with His pain, feeling the full brunt of it. All gods were terrified as Shiva's Thandava had the power to destroy the entire universe. In order to calm the inconsolable Shiva, it is believed that Vishnu, the Indian god of preservation, severed Sati's body into 12 pieces and threw them on earth.

A grief-stricken Shiva, pained by the separation of His love, wandered the various worlds as a nomad, His powers waned. He was inconsolable, pining for His beloved. Only when He was informed by the gods that He was never really separated from His consort, and that soon Sati shall be reborn to re-join Him, was Shiva consoled.

* * * * * * * *

Man is not his body. His body is perishable every lifetime, and every cell in the body is replaced every few weeks in a constant cycle of elimination and renewal. Man is that conscious being who has hitched a ride in that unconscious body for a meagre lifetime. It is to this unconscious body that the five senses belong. By knowing that worldly experiences are merely the satiation of these sensations, and hence are not the true longing of man's true self, by knowing that physical death can take nothing away from the soul's aspiration, man knows his authentic self. To know his soul apart from his physical self is his first step towards authenticity.

In the physical world, being authentic means recognizing man's true nature and living that nature. Where life is rooted in a 'doing' reality, where achievement and over achievement are the norms for success, this is far from easy, for the energy of the current times is mostly geared to the quantum of the 'doing' against which man is weighed. The 'being' has got buried under the weight of this judgment and reproaches of the world around. To break free from this energy and 'be' himself involves paddling upstream against a rushing current, which takes the Mature Masculine all the will and resources of the inner voice. Living in alignment with his inner voice involves digging deep within to seek out the divine voice of the soul, while evading the trap laid by the louder more enticing inner voice of the ego. The ego will tempt him towards 'doing' because in the 'doing' lies the validation and approval it seeks to inflate its ´I-dentification´. It is the way of the immature masculine to live in alignment with the inner voice of the ego which solicits the ´I-dentification´ of adolescence. To minimize the weightage of the 'doing' is to step into realism, leaving the illusions of the mind behind, seeking as a Mature Masculine to emulate the meditative mendicant that Shiva was.

When man has chosen to consider any incongruity with the voice of his inner self a failure, he has chosen to become the champion of authenticity. For, the voice of the divine inner self speaks what is most natural to himself, while always taking into consideration the welfare of other beings, animate and inanimate. Into its synthesis, the divine inner self has incorporated the past, present and the future, the I and the us, the form and the matter, the body and the non-body. It is all-knowing and is never wrong, because in its most unadulterated form, it is but only a channel for the Supreme. To honour that inner voice may involve saying no to the external voices of society which are often in deep conflict with it. It takes a mature masculine to uphold the virtue of the voice of his divine inner self even at the cost of disagreeing with another's viewpoint or perspective. He recognizes that he is actually saying yes to the voice of his divine inner self each time he says no to the external voices haunting him incessantly. In that yes, the Mature Masculine reflects the Supreme in his life. He has become aligned between the voice of his divine inner self and its manifestation in his physical life.

As meant above, being authentic is not being in alignment with man's ego self, rather being in alignment with his highest (divine or soul) self. It means not being man's animal instinctive self, which self is motivated by fear and does not consider anything sinful. The egoistic self is obsessed with its individual and clan interests. In its most primitive expression, that self is only consumed with three pursuits in life; survival, procreation and identity. In contrast to the demands of the egoistic self, man's most authentic self is in pursuit of oneness with all beings and yonder. The Mature Masculine's ability to look beyond himself to bring into his fold all beings, starting from those closest – his friends and family – up until the farthest, beyond caste, creed, class, colour or race, to go beyond inclusiveness to embrace oneness, that is the Mature Masculine being his most authentic self.

The faithful companion for man today as he steps into adulthood seems to be the burden of expectations of parents and society that he carries in his backpack. Even before he has stepped into adulthood, an unsolicited script has already been written for man and thrust upon him, and he is but just a mere actor in that play. He must don a different façade with each act and each stakeholder of his life. This is valid for both genders today, is it not?

Man has moved out of his parents' home, but he still lives the role prescribed often unconsciously by his parents. He has become mobile, but the key to his liberation seems still left under his mother's pillow. He has grown tall, but he chooses to still be trapped in childish roles with his parents. He has recognized his sexuality, but he still seeks approval to be himself. From a place of co-dependence he leans on his woman, lest he should fall and scratch his knee. He is trapped in his need for approval and social acceptance, unlike the *Bhasmeshwar* (one strewn with ash, Shiva) who is at perfect ease being Himself even at the expense of negating socially accepted rituals and behaviours.

As modern man grows further, he cries to be noticed for what he does and what he has in life. He has become the product of everything around him, his experiences, his possessions, his roles, his designations. He has chosen to be yet another white sheep, in fact he expels energy fighting a gruelling war to make sure that he remains congruent with what the world around him aspires him to become. Not only does this leave him worn down and devoid of vitality, but also has he dishonoured his most noble inner voice. Amidst those blaring megaphones of society, the feeble voice of his inner voice gently inviting him to be himself fails to be heard.

Weakness is the effect of the transferring of man's being onto something other than what he is. The more he thinks of things other than what he is, the weaker are also his sense organs, mind and intellect. People have a wrong notion that they become stronger by the possession of a larger quantum of things in the world. Rather, the greater man's reliance on his possessions for self-identity, the weaker is his personality. The more his self-assurance depends on his property, the weaker he is. It is a weak man whose self-identity solely depends upon property to prop it up. The stronger he is, the lesser is the need of any kind in this world.

Self-love goes hand-in-hand with authenticity. Today man is passionately caught up in the belief that there is always something that can be different – and better - about himself. Such belief bleeds away his self-love. What is better for man is a matter of judgment, however as he starts to peel the layers of pre-conditioning and move out of darkness into light towards greater self-realization, he is uncovering the inherent potentialities of his Soul. This is an on-going process. In the pursuit of a greater whole, in the journey towards greater authenticity, man must not condemn himself or judge himself harshly. Unconsciously, he has become habituated to love or dislike himself through observing his parents' love or dislike for themselves. This habit is the darkness that man must choose to escape from to practice self-love. The Mature Masculine recognizes that he is the child of the Infinite, however he bears in him the good and not-so-good, the light and darkness, the gross and the subtle, love and fear, all in fair proportions. He surrenders into the knowing that for this moment of time, he is the perfect blend of all the elements of creation. He knows of the transient nature of his body and mind, and that tomorrow he will graduate to a new perfect blend. This incessant process of amalgamation and re-amalgamation will only terminate when the *Atman* (the individual Soul) becomes one with the *Paramatman* (the Cosmic Soul), and in that knowingness the Mature Masculine finds his self-love.

When the Mature Masculine realizes that his worldly fulfilment is only but *Maya* (an illusion), he understands that the happiness originating from all that is external to him is fleeting in nature. Any dysfunctional dependence that man has for fulfilment from external loci is only the yearning of the ego, and the many masks that he wears to solicit or acquire the external source of such fulfilment serves only an impermanent purpose. With resolve the Mature Masculine chooses to tear down those masks, even as he is aware that in the absence of those masks he may initially feel confused. As he peels off those layers of the crust of un-authenticity around his being, at first he finds himself exposed and vulnerable. But as he reaches into his very own essence, he starts to notice that the heaviness of his mask is now replaced by the lightness of his true self. The lack of radiance of his aura is being replaced by the sparkle of his soul escaping through his eyes. As an avatar of the *Sadjyota* (the Eternally Radiant One, Shiva), the expressions of his true nature glow. He notices that the world around him views him with admiration. Those who look at him now look up to him.

* * * * * * * *

As the Mature Masculine continues on his path of authenticity, he reinforces this great expression of his by asking himself daily;

- ✓ Do I put a premium on my life of 'doing' or on my life of 'being'?
- ✓ How often do I honor the preference of my innervoice over the preference of all those external voices trying to impose their preferences upon me?
- ✓ Am I in a parent-child relationship with my mother, or am I in an adult-adult relationship with her?
- ✓ Do I accept and love myself for who I am, or do I consider myself imperfect and judge myself harshly?

15. PURPOSEFULNESS: THE MATURE MASCULINE BEING ON HIS PATH

"Atma mokshartham jagathitaya cha"
[To liberate oneself and serve the world]
(Shaivaite proverb)

As it says in the Upanishads (some of the ancient Indian texts); "Bahudha chakti yogat varnananekan nihitartho dadhati."
[By His many-sided activity, which radiates in all directions, does He fulfil the inherent want of His different creatures.]

"Just as the poet in his poem, the artist in his art, the brave man in the output of his courage, the wise man in his discernment of truths, ever seeks expression in their several activities, so the knower of Brahma (Supreme Consciousness) - in his everyday work - seeks to give expression to the Infinite. That inherent want is his true self, and it is the deepest yearning of his soul to give himself in service. In so many ways, in so many forms, little and big, in truth, in beauty, he dedicates himself. He dedicates, for without dedicating how could he live his purpose."
(Adopted from Sadhana: Rabindranath Tagore)

* * * * * * * *

During man's upbringing, when he comes in touch with delicious sweet sensorial experiences like taste, smell, touch, beauty, etc. he develops attraction towards them. His sensorial pursuits seem like a great big candy store, it grabs his imagination, fires up his desires, enslaves his senses, and his craving mind runs after it through his life henceforth. He comes to believe that these pursuits are the aim of his existence.

After the Mature Masculine has lived through his sensorial experiences, he ponders deeply on whether there is more to life beyond this consumption and eschewing. His spotlights get trained on larger questions of life. He asks if his life was just another quirky coincidence, another faint blip on the radar screen of the Infinite. As he realizes that there ought to be more to life than is visible to the naked eye, he senses his dissatisfaction with the status quo. A blaring urge gushes through him making him restless. He opens himself to the force of his discontentment, inviting his restlessness to show him the way towards his reason for birth. He scrutinizes his various roles as a son, husband, father, employee and friend, yearning all the while to find justifications for the life lived this far.

Doubts enter his mind as his heart declares that if he were to die today, the yet un-cherished expressions of love that he was meant to embody remain un-manifested. His soul reminds him that he has not yet scripted and sculpted the legacy that he was chosen to leave behind. He would not have left this place better than it was when he arrived. Unlike neon lamps in the night horizon, his innate nature has not been on display yet. Against the push and pull of confused employer, sceptical friends and nervous spouse, he asks himself, “Why am I born?” Thus begins his pursuit for his *Dharma*.

Dharma is the innermost nature, the essence, the implicit truth, of all things. It is the ultimate purpose that is working in man’s self. But this *Dharma* - which is the truth in him - is not apparent, because it is inherent. So much so, that it has also been held that sinfulness is the nature of man, and only by the special grace of the Supreme can he be saved. Does the ocean need an exceptional grace to express its waves? Does the tree need a miracle medicine to grow towards the light? Does the river need a special dispensation to flow down from the mountains? Does a new-born need a divine intervention to be in union with its mother? Does a seed need the intervention of a special force to express its 'treeness'?

All the miracles that a seed need to sprout are already inherent within it. All the gifts that a seed needs to beam at the sun are contained within the seed. All the intelligence that the seed needs to flourish into a tree and bear its flowers and fruits are innate to its nature. Through its smell, or its colour, or its texture, or its design, or its taste, man cannot determine the *Dharma* of the seed. By leaving the seed in unfertile soil, away from water and nourishment, away from warmth, leaving it to rot, its *Dharma* does not express itself. It is when the seed is laid in fertile soil, with warmth and wetness, that its *Dharma* becomes evident. Similarly, all beings – animate and inanimate – express their *Dharma* when in their ideal natural conditions.

Manava Dharma (the life purpose of a human being) consists of two essentials. These essentials are elegantly encapsulated in the following text;
"Atma mokshartham Jagat Hitayacha."
[Self-Realization and Service to Beings]

Self-realization involves *Vistara* (self-expansion), that is expanding man's awareness of himself. Beyond the gross body, there exists within man subtle and causal realms which supersede and govern his physical existence. In these realms, he is united with all, he is non-perishable and eternal. Each man is also endowed with a unique gift with the purpose of proceeding on his path of *Dharma*. This gift is a composition of various talents, experiences and skills that is specific in its mix for each. Applying that unique gift involves becoming aware of it, that awareness being his first step on his path of *Dharma*. Living his *Dharma*, man falls in tune with the Supreme will, man and Nature falls in step, and there arises bliss in man.

Seva (selfless service to all beings) involves man giving himself totally into the welfare of all beings. Man must transcend the give-and-take paradigm to embody the spirit of giving. Embodied in the mind-set of tireless acquisition, man has forgotten that in order to truly receive matter along with its meaning he must disconnect his expectations for rewards from his act of giving. *Seva* is giving from a place of detachment to outcomes. More of this will come in a later chapter.

The Mature Masculine's *Dharma* is his impetus to move through the journey of life, it is his source of meaning and joy. His *Dharma* sucks away the inconveniences and impediments that the present throws at him, and graciously he seeks to embrace those with the knowingness that these inconveniences and impediments are nothing but tests on his path of *Dharma*. His purposefulness becomes the soothing balm to the battle wounds that he carries in his noble pursuit. As Shiva said;
"Parishrama vina karyasiddhirbhavati durlabha"[9]
[Without purposeful effort, success in any field of activity is impossible].

In the history of humanity we have seen the living seed in man sprout. We have seen the great purpose in us taking shape in the lives of our greatest men, sprouting from the seed and transforming themselves into a noble spiritual shoot, growing up into the air and light, and branching out in all directions. Purposeful effort has entailed sacrifice to attain this fulfilment, breaking free of the bondages imposed upon them by history, circumstances, society or time. The higher nature in the Mature Masculine always seeks for something which transcends itself and yet is its deepest truth; which claims all its sacrifice, yet makes this sacrifice its own recompense. This is man's *Dharma*, man's inherent aspiration, man's purpose for existence, and man's body is the wagon that carries this sacrifice to its fruition.

Vision is inherent in *Dharma*, and he who is ensconced in *Dharma* is fully tuned into his intuition. When one inserts his hand into a beehive and grabs the queen bee, all the bees follow. Likewise, when man uses his intuition to illuminate his path, vision automatically appears.

As Allama Prabhu, an Indian poet once sang of Shiva;
"Looking for your light,
I went out:
it was like the sudden dawn
of a million million suns,
a ganglion of lightnings
for my wonder.
O Lord of Caves,
if you are light,
there can be no metaphor."

For genuine mystics, light (otherwise vision) is not a mere concept; it is the luminosity of the visionary, Shiva - which is clearly what Allama Prabhu is describing with this verse. This light is perceived as being a living radiance that permeates everything, everywhere, always. It is a radiance that outshines everything "like the sudden dawn of a million million suns." This light is immediately understood to be the beacon to all things beyond sight, the foundation on which the path to oneness with the Absolute is built. The sense of boundaries and separation, long taken for granted by the mind as the fundamental nature of existence, suddenly seems illusory, for this vision shines through all people, things and time.

As a visionary, Shiva saw of a future beyond division. He saw all beings as one only differentiated by their *Samskaras* (the burden of consequences of one's good and bad actions), each being at the perfect place where they are meant to be today.

The Mature Masculine recognizes that his vision originates from the oneness of his own Self with that of the all-knowing Source. Through his union, he taps into the Source to see into the yonder, beyond time, space and persons. It is his imperative to tap into it, and let it shine its light upon the paths that take all forward. Vision inspires action as it did when seven thousand years ago society responded to Shiva's call for community building. Shiva declared;
"Atmagotram parityajya Shivagotram pravishata" [9]
[Give up the small clan, enter the community of Shiva].

The Mature Masculine inspires and mobilizes those around him with his vision. His vision unites intentions and bonds hearts. It gives direction and focus.

* * * * * * * *

As the Mature Masculine continues being on his path of purposefulness, he asks himself daily;

- ✓ Is there more to my life than my worldly life of the material and the mundane?
- ✓ Knowing that there are no accidents in the universe, why am I born?
- ✓ What is it that I am passionate about that is greater than myself?

16.HIS SIMPLE-HEARTEDNESS THAT MAKES HIM VISIBLE

"Jai Gauri Shankara Jai Vishwanath
Jai Parvati Pati Bhole Nath
Bhole Nath Bhole Nath
Jai Parvati Pati Bhole Nath"
[Glory to Gauri, the consort of Shiva, Glory to the Lord of the Universe,
Glory to the husband of Parvati, the Simple Lord, Who fulfils all desires.
The Simple Lord, the Simple Lord,
Glory to the Husband of Parvati, the Simple Lord, Who fulfils all desires]
(Devotional song of Shiva)

Shiva is often called 'Bhole Nath'. In Sanskrit 'Bhole' means innocent, simple-hearted, unsophisticated. Some also take the name to mean the Good One, or the Pure One. Shiva is the embodiment of the highest expression of simple-heartedness. His simple-heartedness is an expression of integrity. He is also lovingly called 'Ashutosha' (One who is easily pleased). In Indian mythology, Shiva is believed to have a white complexion. The white complexion is His silent teaching that one should sport a pure heart, entertain pure thoughts, express pure words, embody pure deeds and should be free from crookedness, cunning, jealousy, hatred, etc.

A little love, a little devotion, a little allegiance, a little perseverance on the path of Dharma and Shiva gives boons out to His devotees quite readily. There is an amusing tale related to Shiva's simple-heartedness. Once Bhasmasura - a demon with the ambition of ruling the entire universe - propitiated Shiva. Shiva appeared and granted Bhasmasura a boon of his choice. Bhasmasura wished that he be given such power through which anyone on whose head he would place his hand, would turn to ashes. Shiva innocently granted him the boon and no sooner had he done so, Bhasmasura immediately decided to make Shiva his first victim. He chased Shiva endlessly to turn him to ashes. Vishnu (the preserver God of Indian mythology), decided to help Shiva out of the unpleasant situation he had created for himself. Vishnu assumed the form of an enchantress named Mohini, and seduced Bhasmasura into joining her for a dance thus getting his attention diverted from Shiva. She then fooled Bhasmasura into placing his hand on his own head thus killing himself.

* * * * * * * *

Caught in the trap of 'I-ness', the world may seem to be against him. Madly he fights for the varied objects of the world, for therein he perceives his guarantee for survival and procreation. He sees himself as an isolated unit in constant battle with the elements of Nature and with mankind. Led by his instincts, these external battles are but an echo of his inner reality.

When man has disconnected from his innate essence of oneness with all, he starts to look at others through the lens of separation. The pureness and innocence that were the hallmarks of the pristine child within become shrouded in the darkness of impurity. In his sight, the negatives in others magnify. The blinding rays of the negatives leave the goodness in others in its shadows, and he turns blind to goodness. His negativity gradually metastasizes within him to become one with his egoic nature. Like ripples of waves propagating through still water, it resolutely encompasses man's life until his thoughts, deeds and actions all become expressions of that negativity. Slowly but steadily with time, his negativity becomes the quintessence of his existence. And like cancer spreading through the body, this negativity creeps into all relationships. The disease that grew roots in one domain of life is now spreading its branches within all other domains; his family, friendships, neighbours, work, society, acquaintances. It becomes unstoppable and all-consuming. When the heat and motion of this blinding energy distracts him from all sides, he can neither give nor receive anything truly. He has become oblivious to the fact that he has created that hurt within him, and any external actor to his pain were only triggers, witnesses and victims to the unfolding drama of negativity within him.

As man shifted consciousness from being a brute to a more subtle being, his awareness developed beyond his instincts. His sphere of 'I-ness' expanded beyond himself. It is as recent as seven thousand years ago when the sphere of 'I-ness' expanded to include the concept of family. With that advent, purity of thoughts for others started to germinate. That which is one in him, ever seeking unity in love, started to shine its radiance.

For many, pure thoughts, words and conduct depend on time, space and person. The ego discriminates and determines the occasion for the higher self in him to express itself. This is the nature or the impure mind. For such a mind, purity is relative to the external reality of an individual. However, it should not be so. How can a conduct be pure if it changes with circumstances? The locus for pure conduct is internal, that is within oneself. To the Mature Masculine, he himself is the locus for pure conduct, and he maintains no discrimination as to the time, place and person when he chooses to live the oneness within him. Pureness of thought, word and deed is not rationed based on external circumstances, for the path of purity is the path of simple-heartedness.

The Mature Masculine realizes that the supreme state of pureness is achieved when his thoughts, words and deeds are constantly and consistently pure. Irrespective of the external circumstance, his practices of pure conduct in the physical world involves refraining from meting out injustice and taking advantage of others materially, while in the mental realm he is the fountain of kindness, compassion and universalism. He aspires only for the good of others, and his higher self, seeking its counterpart in others, gives the benefit of doubt to all beings. Through a constant process of conscious practice, he aspires to be wedded to pureness in thoughts, words and deed until he has reached a stage of automatism where all that originates from him are pure.

The ultimate sign of his embrace of pureness comes when even in his dreams – when he is asleep – his thoughts are pure. This is evidence that through his disciplined spiritual practice, he has mastered his mind, and he has harmonized all warring elements within the walls of his mind. He has unified those that are apart, all his isolated impressions of truth have metamorphosed themselves into wisdom, and all his momentary impulses of heart have found their completion in love. At the level at which all his thoughts and deeds have united themselves inseparably in an internal harmony and pureness, he has found within him that which is truly innate; the Mature Masculine.

It is man's constant endeavour to harmonize the heterogeneous complexity of outward materials by an inner adjustment. Herein lies the irony of man. On the one hand, his lower self is in a constant pursuit of fulfilment of his illegitimate needs, needs created by the ego. As needs diversify, so does the complexity of man's external environment of concern. On the other hand is the yearning of the higher self within man to bring into alignment and harmony all internal and external faculties of his being. This swing of the pendulum from one extreme to the other is the cosmic dance of the eternal and ephemeral. He must master this dance if he were to attain self-realization.

Complexities exist within, and are created because man's ego comes into play. Humans are the only being - among the 3 billion identified species - who is capable of using its ego to go against the flow of Nature. The ego in us has come to expect that the laws of Nature should be held in abeyance for our own convenience. This expectation has forced humans to decimate his environment and impose upon the will of Nature. Constant dissonance between human and Nature has become the norm, this external dissonance simply being an echo of the complexities that reside within contemporary humans.

The antidote to complexities is surrender. What does it mean to surrender? It means to emulate the state of being of other beings that exist alongside man, and giving Nature space to compose Its symphony and conducts Its orchestra. When man tunes into his intuition, he can play the same notes as Nature because Nature shares Its tunes with man through the voice of his intuition. It is said of Shiva;

"Bahudha chakti yogat varnananekan nihitartho dadhati."

[By His multi-pronged activity which radiates in all directions, does He fulfil the inherent want of His different creatures.]

The simple-heartedness of the Mature Masculine is to forego his self-gratification, his pride of possession, his insolent alienation of Nature's heart. He operates from a place of non-resistance, and rather than be guided by the ego, he plays the tune of his intuition. He surrenders in the knowlngness that Nature's law cannot be set aside, and in this knowledge he becomes strong. For Nature's laws are not something apart from him, they are his own. It will thwart him where his existence is misaligned with the current of things, but It will prop him up where he is one with It.

Indulgence in falsehood out of personal interest or ingrained habit is not an attribute of the simple-hearted. As is stated in the *Upanishads* (some of the ancient Indian texts);
"Dharmah sah na satyamasti"
[Where there is no truth, there is no life-purpose].

Pureness and innocence is the quintessence of truth. Seen through the eyes and altitude of a child, truth acquires its divine meaning. To the child, it is the melody that guides the dance, the life-force that drives Nature, the essence that cultivates love, the soil that sprouts compassion. It is the action of the mind and the use of speech in the spirit of welfare[9]. It is the foundation on which the multi-dimensional growth and expression of *Dharma* (life purpose; innate nature) takes place.

In contrast, the logical man equates truth to facts. In his linear brain cause and effect must connect, patterns need to correlate, and facts become his scriptures. In his attachment to facts, he becomes oblivious to beings, and their pain turns irrelevant to him. In his lack of communion with the essence of other beings, his pursuit is designed to seek hollow wins or artificial righteousness. He lives robed in the illusory veil of facts, being content on an imaginary pedestal of self-righteousness, forgetful that facts that do not serve the welfare of all is not truth.

And when ego and logic gets wedded, man's mind swings to another extreme. Man feels the need to inflate his personality so that others are confounded and stupefied, he wants to be noticed as being unique, different. The ego yearns to be recognized, it thirsts for appreciation, and to quench it, it seeks the truth that serves itself best at that moment. Neither is this the same as adjusting the fact to upkeep the welfare of all.

The Mature Masculine displays courage and embodies a deep sense of awareness and compassion to exercise truth. Being on his path of *Dharma* (life purpose; innate nature), he is a champion of truth, where necessary re-forming facts to defend and nourish the welfare of the world.

* * * * * * * *

As the Mature Masculine continues living his pureness and innocence, he reflects on the following questions as part of his daily practice of simple-heartedness;

- ✓ Does pureness in thought, word and deed come to me naturally, or is it still a result of conscious effort?
- ✓ Am I able to feel the same pureness of thought, word and deed for those I dislike as for those I love (irrespective of whether they like me or dislike me, irrespective of whether they hurt me or serve me)?
- ✓ Am I able to surrender control of my extermal faculties and instead be led by my intuition?
- ✓ Knowing that Nature speaks to me through my intuition, am I able to relinquish control of the ego and surrender into the will of Nature?
- ✓ Do I feel my child-like innocence in my practice of truthfulness?

17.LIVING IN THE EQUANIMOUS PRESENT

"O' my dear friend,
let us celebrate this very moment that is the present.
For this present moment holds in its womb the secrets of the past
and the hopes of a glorious future.

The pulsating joy of our connectedness with the Infinite
in the undying spirit of the present.
How blessed we are to be living in it!
Let us learn from the past and move on.

Holding the 'flame of a glorious future for all beings',
let us kindle this candle
of concern and compassion
for generations yet to come.

Let us celebrate the present with our infinite love –
And in this celebration, let everyone join us:
Young, old, little and big.....
And even the stars, galaxies and distant worlds."[35]

* * * * * * * *

What is the past and the future? Just *Maya* (an illusion). The past is nothing but the present already expressed. It has come and gone. The past is but soft imprints left on the sandy dunes of our minds. With the winds of time, slowly but steadily they fade, to leave room for more presents to leave their stories. Now it only exists as a figment in the mind, memories in your brain cells. The past is a relative concept. What is past to me may not be past to you. It may be very much your present. In that spirit, the past is attached to the present, and it is only as good as its application in the present. If man does not watch out, the past cannibalizes the experience of the present. "The past is like a thief, it will steal your present and future," a teacher once reminded me.

The future is just a mirage that we set our mind on. It does not exist except in man's expectations. As transient as expectations are, so short-lived is the future. When the present or the past does not yield the joy he seeks, he flees into the future to somehow find his peace in a reality that is elusive, but worthy of pursuit. Similar to the past, the future is related to the present, however only through man's thoughts, aspirations and intentions. Only a future that lives in detached goodness in his inner reality is worth its space in mind. As with the past, what is future for me may not be future for you, which makes the future illusory.

When man let's his mind dictate his existence over his heart, he finds himself living in the past or in the future. He becomes oblivious to the present. This moment that you experience, where you, the book, the words and the feelings exist, that is the present. When you are one with all that is at this moment, time and space disappears. You become oblivious to the daylight or the night, cold or warmth, indoors or outdoors, upstairs or downstairs.

Man is unconsciously tuned to run away from pain and gravitate towards pleasure. He has learned to crave for what he likes, and to feel aversion for that which he does not. He has turned into a polarized being, creating overpowering interpretations of events around him and his pursuits. He has created his own language for events and pursuits, and this language has imprisoned him into a pattern of feelings that controls his reality. He has learned to call sunny weather great weather and clouded and rainy weather as lousy weather. He dances and exalts when it is sunny and warm, and inversely he feels helplessly drawn into depression when it is clouded and raining. His polarized craving and aversion has programmed his biology to respond in ways that has turned him into a victim rather than be the naturally, intuitively and universally connected being that he actually is.

The inner struggle of man is akin to the pendulum that swings between craving on the one extreme and aversion on the other. At the central point of the path of the pendulum is that place of equanimity that is the coming together of that which is craving and that which is detachment, of that which is aversion and that which is allowing, of that which is the yearning of his human self and that which is the noble aspiration of his higher self, of that which is urgent and that which is important, of that which he desires and that which he wills, of that which is sensually pleasurable and that which is purposefully heartfelt.

Hence the saying in the *Upanishads* (some of the ancient Indian texts);
"Vartamanesu varteta"
[Live in the present.]

In his practice of living in the equanimous present, the Mature Masculine is in absolute awareness of all there is, the sensations within the body, the thoughts, the heartbeat, the activities in the stomach, the pulsating body, the throbbing of muscles, the aches, the itches. The smells, the distant sounds, the sensations on the skin, the hues and shades of lights, the subtle colours, all become evident. Amongst these festivals of Nature's events, he notices the reverberating sounds of silence, a quiet where there is only himself in fast communion with all there is. As he melds into the silence, the smile on his face slowly appears, time disappears, sensations become ethereal, and a peace settles upon himself. Like a balloon floating in the wind, a lightness envelops him, the tightness of his material self is replaced by the flow of the subtle self. He might feel a whistle escape his lips, a boisterous laughter breakout through the body, or the pouring tears of joy and gratitude for the gift of receiving without asking, of having without seeking, of 'being' without 'doing'. A deep understanding for all actors in life floods the mind, compassion for all beings courses through the body, love overflows. In that moment, Nature's *Dharma* (purpose of being) is fulfilled. This is the experience of the equanimous present.

The Mature Masculine's conduct in the equanimous present will be examined in the next chapter.

*   *   *   *   *   *   *   *

As the Mature Masculine continues living in his equanimous present, he reinforces his daily practice by reflecting on the following questions;

- ✓ Do I notice my mind drift into the past or future, or am I here in the here-and-now?
- ✓ Do I take enough time out to simply be with my body, its sensations and in observation of my thoughts?
- ✓ To what extent am I able to detach myself from craving and aversion for people and things, and be in equanimity in my everyday life?

18.MAN'S DETACHMENT FROM SELF-ENHANCING OUTCOMES

"You assumed the form of light,
Brahma and Vishnu failed
To measure Thee,
Thou art Infinity and Eternity."

(Sarvalinga Stava)

Something must remain after the 'Dissolution' of the universes, and the serpent Shesha – known in Indian Mythology as the god of the snakes - is the principle of the 'Remainder' of destroyed universes. In the Mahabharata (an ancient Indian epic), Shesha is portrayed as a great being who has become a penance-practicing ascetic. His austere penances have brought him to an exalted state, and to the attention of the God of creation, Brahma.

Shesha is offered by Brahma the boon of eternal paradise, instead it wants to rise above the jealously and envy which characterize his brothers. Shesha asks only that his 'heart always delights in virtue and joy', and to fill his eyes with the sight of Shiva's dance. Pleased with Shesha's selflessness, Shiva appears as His immanent Self and enlightens Shesha on the wisdom of the universe. Shesha is offered the boon of being born as a human to be able to witness Shiva's cosmic dance of ecstasy forever.

* * * * * * * *

Man's greatest responsibility is in being himself; that is the design of Nature. Like the mother experiences her bliss in her union with her new-born, it is in man's innateness that he experiences his blissful union with the Absolute. However, when he is attached to the future, his innate nature is obscured. Like iron particles being subject to the force field of a magnet when in its presence, man who is consumed by his future is drawn by the gravitational pull of his future. The closer the iron particles are to the magnet, the farther they are from its own state of equilibrium. Similarly, man who is deeply attached to the future is farther away from his innate nature. His true nature is on display only when the tension exerted by the force fields of his attachment to outcomes is taken away.

Man is trapped in forms. This is true not only for his physical reality of existence - like his body - but also for his views. He is limited to seeing things in forms. And in seeing the contours of everything in Nature, he notices only the separateness among things. To recognize the oneness of all there is within and around him, he must practice seeing the underlying essence - the matter - over the form.

Man is a microcosm of the universe; he is a mirror that reflects the entirety of the universe, within him resides all the divinity that is contained in Nature, and he is infinite within the confines of his human existence. To recognize that enormity that resides within him is the first step towards transcending his false notion of separateness from *Parama Purusha* (Supreme Consciousness), and looking at all animate and inanimate as a simple extension of his being. The notes and the melody of the cosmic orchestra of the Supreme Consciousness is already defined, and man being one of the notes, his outcome is already designed. His choice is limited to clearing the air passage so that his expression – being that note - is its fullest, his most divine. When man oversteps his limits and orchestrates the outcomes, he generates local optimums, optimums that suit himself and his own. Through resolutely being his own innate self, it is the Mature Masculine's constant endeavour to align his intentions with that of the Supreme Consciousness, so that he can become Its instrument to sculpt the global optimum, an optimum that brings to him the greatest outcome.

Deeds man must have, for only in the act of 'doing' does he manifest his infinite energy whose bliss is in cognition and operation.
It is said;
"ShivaShakti vibhajana jayaté srishtikalpana"
[When Shiva and *Shakti* are separated, the imagination of creation is aroused.]

The Supreme Consciousness – being the amalgamation of Shiva (the Cognitive Faculty) and *Shakti* (the Operative Faculty) - manifests everything in the universe through the application of both these faculties, and humanity being the reflection of the Supreme Consciousness, is a medium through which creation occurs. In being an instrument of the Infinite that propels the act of 'doing', the Mature Masculine lives his bliss of being on purpose.

In every act of life, man must bring his 'being' in alignment with his 'doing'. Of all beings of Nature, man - with his superior intellect - is the only being who does what he does, not just out of instinct or need. He is not content with his 'doingness' that is only driven by compulsion. Rather, the fullest expression of his inner divine displays itself in his acts driven by his heart's deepest longing. With this thought in mind, the Supreme Consciousness has endowed him with unique gifts that find their fullest expression in the manifestation of his heart's longing. When his 'doing' reflects his heart's longing, he is passionate; he radiates his fullest joy, his glory shines incessantly, fellow beings are inspired, Nature follows, and his reason for existence is fulfilled. However, there is a precondition to man's 'doing' radiating his fullest joy, and that is to relinquish any desire he may carry for outcomes. When man is consumed by outcomes, it is only his ego exerting itself in self-reinforcing ways. Like the passing of dark clouds in the sky, the meaning then becomes transient, the satisfaction fleeting.

When man lusts for the outcomes of his deeds, all kinds of things go wrong. For example, he is consumed by his yearning to win at all costs. Like a hamster on the hamster-wheel in a perpetual run, his yearning turns into an end in itself. He becomes territorial in his everyday life, be it in the supermarket queue, waiting to board a train, in how he places his fence around his home, in every walk of life. We continue to witness countries divide where global unions should be forged, and on-going ideological warfare where unity must be preached.

Winning always involves a reference, either external or internal, that is, there is always an external or internal target against which man is in a match. He takes winning and losing seriously. When he wins, he rejoices as if he has subdued some dark forces that had come to haunt him, and when he loses he sulks, he becomes disappointed and disillusioned. It is the nature of the Mature Masculine to become referenceless, becoming free from external or internal targets, and in that referencelessness he becomes eternally victorious.

Further, man's relentless pursuit of outcomes traps him in the illusion of separateness which prompts him to take advantage of others, to impose himself upon others, to exert force and administer his power over others, to secure his benefits at the detriment of others. This separateness is created by the ego. Living in the illusion of separateness, is to cling desperately - and often unconsciously - to his separate ego identity. In doing so, he is incapable of enjoying this divine game called Nature. He relates to others through fear, guilt or shame, and in that energy field the 'other' is the cause for the effect that he feels. The 'other' is the perpetrator and he falsely feels the victim.

To transcend separateness is to master the ego. As the Mature Masculine masters his ego, he practices not to separate himself from the other and himself from Nature, and he starts on a path of greater self-realization. This path brings greater command over himself, it frees him from anxiety associated with uncertainties related to the future, and propels him towards his highest life purpose. He sees everything with compassion and his mastery starts to radiate. He is able to allow the outcomes of his action, and in this allowing he finds his purpose and joy.

The Mature Masculine melds into the experience of oneness with his act of 'doing', completely being in the present, oblivious to the past or future. In that oneness, his heart's longing becomes the glue between man and mission, time and space disappears, thoughts dissolve into void, until matter and energy reaches its union in bliss without an external reference. He settles into his 'doing' reassured that the design of the Supreme has allocated the deserving reward for his act, and every act for him is a *Seva*, a selfless service of equanimous goodness that makes him one with the activity of the Infinite.

He recognizes that detachment from outcomes does not mean that he does not have goals and intentions for the future. Rather, he sets goals and intentions with a pure heart, with passion - coming from the whole being - and with detachment. Being in awareness of his goals and intentions, not from a place of victim hood and attachment, rather as the witness from a place of self-mastery is the nature of the Mature Masculine. In the Mature Masculine's actions with no attachment to outcomes he is releasing himself from the bondages of *Karma* (past good or bad actions leading to one's current experiences of joy or sorrow). As the *Upanishads* say about the detachment to outcomes;
"Yadyat karma prakurvita tadbrahmani samarpayet"
[Whatever works thou doest, consecrate them to Brahma.]

As the Mature Masculine is depleting his old karmic account through his 'doing', through the detachment of outcomes he is accumulating no further karmic debts that will continue to trap him in this otherwise perpetual cycle of life and death.

* * * * * * * *

In his daily practice of detaching from self-enhancing outcomes, the Mature Masculine reflects on the following questions;

- ✓ What I am doing now, am I doing it out of the pure pleasure of the act or out of my expectation of a desired outcome?
- ✓ Am I postponing or not undertaking an act because I fear the outcome might not be what I had hoped for?
- ✓ Do I find me comparing myself with others, or being consumed by illusory targets that I have set for myself?
- ✓ Am I surrendered in the knowing that I have given my best in what I do, and whatever outcome appears is the best for me?

19.PLAYFULNESS: THE LIGHTENING SPIRIT THAT COMMANDS

"Amid the flowers of His creation (Prakriti), He lingers in a kiss.
Blinded by their beauty, He rushes, He frolics, He dances, He whirls.
He is all rapture, all bliss, in this play (Lila).
In consciousness alone, in love alone, The Spirit learns the nature of His divine Being.
Divinely playing in the multiplicity of forms, He comprehends Himself."
(Unknown)

It is often difficult for some to understand this playful side of Shiva. Indeed, because Shiva is popularly known as 'The Destroyer', His presence is often portrayed as being terrible and horrific to he who does not recognize his own self. After all, man's self is nothing but a reflection of His Self. Shiva's dance creates the impression of 'Maya' (illusion) which bewilders man's ego and causes forgetfulness of the 'Absolute Truth'. However, all existence is finite, and whatever has been displayed will be dissolved back into the divine essence of 'Brahman' (Cosmic Consciousness). At the end of each Universal Cycle, called the 'Mayayuga' or the Great Eon, it is believed that Shiva destroys all that has been created. Little does humanity realize that Shiva's furious destruction of the Universe is a blessing to the existing beings, merging all souls in oneness into 'Brahman' (Cosmic Consciousness). For the wise and the knowing, this act of destruction secretly heralds the possibility for renewal and regeneration. Something new, in the seer or the seen, always emerges from the waning of the old.

Thus, as man peels the veil of illusion away, he realizes that Shiva's dancing spins with joy and seduction. His dancing makes light of the fear of finality, it toys with the Truth that when it comes to His creation, there are no absolutes. He is the only Absolute. What may seem as an ending to the mortal self is after all only a trick of the light, a shift of playful feet, a change of tune, another turning of the wheel of life. The future is always contained in the present, and the past comes round again and again. It is all in there. Shiva's dance is merely existence at play.

* * * * * * * *

Playfulness is the escape from the ego. Playfulness and ego do not mix as oil and water does not, for the underlying spirit of both are diametrically opposite. While the ego aspires for the 'I' identification, playfulness is about melding into oneness all the inner faculties of an individual with the external space. In pure play, the external - which is just an extension of man's emotions, experiences and sensations - becomes one with his inner self. Boundaries disappear. While the ego controls man's reality by using time as a whip, playfulness dissolves time into non-existence. How often have you heard one say, "I was so absorbed in this game that I didn't know how time flew by!" This transcendence of time is the exalting experience of playfulness.

Further, the ego uses the references of our past to create reservations in the present and anxiety for the future. Man's ego is the repository of all the collective traumas of our past. It is also the storehouse of the hang-ups of his parents and those before. The ego uses those experiences as reference to his every moment-to-moment experience, dragging him away from immersing himself joyfully into the present. After all, if an individual does not exist as an island in all its distinctiveness, where has the ego to go to be free from the vast ocean of oneness?

Playfulness, on the other hand, involves disconnecting from the past and future, and becoming one with the present. There is no past or future to take man back to reason. Along with his 'adult' self, logic dissolves and joyous overflow of energy takes over. This is *Lila nyaya*, the logic of playfulness.

We notice this immersion in kids when they play. Every game is a new one, and every game has a new script. New rules are made on the spot, and any historic references remain hidden in history. Playfulness is in the imagination, and roles are not confined to the straitjacket of the limited physical reality like individual bodies, sexes, size, weight or skin colour. Kids transcend the physical plane to the world of the surreal where reality wanes out to make way for illusions to become reality. In this reality, with one thought or intention every being – real or imaginary - becomes connected in an orchestra of exuberance, colours become brighter, and fragrances are effervescent. The Mature Masculine is aware of this truth and is open to evolve the *Lila* (the divine play) into infinite possibilities.

The Mature Masculine recognizes that every moment will pass, and together with the moment will disappear the experience of the moment as well. The moment may leave a tiny impression in some recess of the mind. But that is all. So there is no point taking the moment seriously. Once the moment has passed, so has the impression. The Mature Masculine is aware that there is no outcome beyond that impression. Hence his playfulness does not yearn an outcome in the future. The fulfilment of the moment itself is the desired outcome. The path itself is the destination. The activity itself is the catharsis. In that knowing lies the freedom to experience the full will of his inner child.

Living the experience of his inner child does not make the Mature Masculine oblivious to the pain of the other, neither does it make him inaccessible to the sensitivities of the other. His inner child is simply free from the complexities, anxieties and preoccupations of the adult mind, it is simply absorbed in its celebration of the magic of each moment.

To the Mature Masculine, being playful is a sign of personal mastery. He surrenders into the realization that the cosmos is the playing field and he the player. His playfulness is the demonstration of his capacity to effortlessly access the inner child and express it without reservations. It is the expression of the alignment he feels with the flow of Nature, because playfulness indeed is his nature. He submits himself into play with a heart full of love, a joyful mind and a vibrant body.

His ability to be playful is the demonstration that he is not affected by the potential adversities that lie hidden in every event of Nature. Those he leave to the adult mind to worry about. The playful spirit of the Mature Masculine's inner child is captured elegantly by the following passage;

"Can you play if you cry from the wind?
Can you play if you run from the pollens?
Can you play if you worry about the sun?
Can you play if you bother being drenched?

Can you play if you are shy of the dirt?
Can you play if the rough edges bother you?

Can you play if you fear of falling?
Can you play if you worry you will freeze?"

(Unknown)

* * * * * * * *

To anchor his daily practice of accessing his inner child, living his playful nature, and radiating his light joyous spirit, he asks himself;

- ✓ Do I take myself too seriously?
- ✓ How easy is it for me in my daily life to awaken my innerchild and experience its lightness of spirit?
- ✓ Am I able to extract myself from the trap of past preconditioning and future-related concerns, and simply rejoice the joy of the moment?

20.SACRIFICE FOR LEGACY, TO TRANSCEND LIFE AND DEATH

"Shiva Shiva Shivaaya Bhava Bhava Bhavaaya
Hara Hara Hara Hara Shambhoo
Tribhuvana Paalaka Haalahala Dhara Shambho
Om Hara Hara Hara Hara Shambho
Alakha Niranjana Bhava Bhaya Bhanjana
Pranavaakara Shambho
Ganga Dhara Hara Gauri Manohara
Saamba Sadha Shiva Shambho"

[Pray to Lord Shiva, destroyer of all evil, the protector of Three Worlds, the One who swallowed and stored in his neck the dreadful poison which would otherwise have destroyed the whole world. Lord, who is bereft of all attachments, destroys all worldly bonds. Lord of Gauri holds the sacred flow of Ganges in his matted lock and is the very embodiment of primordial sound "Om".]

(Devotional chant of Shiva)

The period of Shiva was believed to be a most turbulent time for the civilization in India. Indian civilization was on a struggle to reconcile the essences of the teachings of the Aryans on the one hand, and the teachings of the indigenous Indians on the other hand. Through His birth, Shiva consecrated the civilization in India, and He spent His whole life to advance the cause of universal welfare. Against the backdrop of distrust, timidity, and antipathy, Shiva wanted to bring all beings to the path of liberation. He wanted all beings to devote to the aim of 'Moksha', salvation.

He recognized that all beings in human form had the capacity to access the most subtle realms of the mind. With that conviction, He was willing to unflinchingly persist, even sacrificing Himself against the ravages of dark forces that are active within the mind. Externally, the dark forces were those beings who wanted to cast the net of their supremacy over others, while internally – within humans – the dark forces were the propensities of the ego which was more fascinated by the passing show of the external world than the wonders of the inner world. Shiva took on the pain and suffering of facing those forces, which internally and externally are mere echoes of each other.

*   *   *   *   *   *   *   *

Following man's purpose requires the greatness born out of sacrifice; sacrifice of himself for others but even further, sacrificing himself for the greater ideal of living his reason to be born. That is what makes him a mature masculine. Sacrificing – for the Mature Masculine - does not mean giving up something. Rather, sacrifice for him is making choices that are beyond the scope of understanding of the limited psyche, a joy that transcends the mundane acquisition, the bliss that is part and parcel of selfless giving. Man is unconsciously aware of his greater self which transcends the limits of his personality, for every man has – sometime or the other – given up something for the sake of another, every man has felt a joy in losing something or putting himself through trouble because it pleased somebody else.

Every man is the chosen one. Within every man resides the unconscious intention to support all beings embody a greater ideal. No man is an accident of Nature, even he who moans that he was conceived due to his parents carelessness. To the naked eye, to the limited human ego, it may seem a careless accident, but even that 'accident' is part of a divine conspiracy. With that knowing life acquires a special relevance. Sacrifice becomes a joyful act of meaning, a fulfilling act of giving. As with the mother of a new born, as with the proud father of his family, as with a devoted being of one's idol, as with the resolute leader of the masses, as with the compassionate caregiver to the ill, sacrifice becomes an end in itself.

To the Mature Masculine, the meaning of such sacrifice is to reach some ultimate truth, some positive ideal, which in its greatness can accept suffering and transmute it into profound all-round peace. He knows that he can never attain true emancipation from suffering by fleeing from it, but rather by building intimacy with suffering until it has moved from the unconscious realm to the conscious and into the light of love.

Legacy – in the sense discussed here - is created when man has given, not when he has taken from the world around, and not when he has attempted to extend his proprietary rights over the world and its beings. It is created when good is set free from the obstruction of the bad. When man's nobility has stirred the human heart to its immense depths, when he has given himself completely to impossible deeds of heroism, when he has revealed to humanity the Infinite which is in all humanity, he has created legacy.

Throughout the sagas of exploitation and suffering of mankind, humanity has witnessed courageous men being the symbol of the fullest expression of the soul. Throughout history, man's mistakes have been by no means small, his failures by no means trifling. His radical and self-serving ideologies have strewn the path of history with agony and devastation, his institutions have been slaughterhouses where humanity and its collective yearning for oneness were butchered. In the midst of it all, like a cold soothing shower on a hot humid day, man's unshakable faith in humanity has shone and shone again. The Mature Masculine through history have not been cowed down by the impediments of life, rather have they held on to life with all their might. Pain and sorrow dismayed them not, and heads held high, these victorious heroes marched through life seeing themselves and showing themselves in increasing resplendence of soul.

We have seen glorious examples in men who have stood up for the welfare of his fellow beings, and to defend and protect the less fortunate in society. Also when the dark forces of colonialism exerted itself upon humanity, or when the scourge of racial discrimination was rampant, man's highest self has risen to declare its presence, to exhibit its beauty, to demonstrate its innate goodness, and to vindicate the very soul of our collective consciousness. In righteous anger, it has raised its voice, demanded its dignity, and staked its claim upon the collective goodness that is human's nature. And after the wrong was righted, man's highest self put to rest the same energy that redressed the social malice lest it should appear again to turn the victims into aggressors. In his condoning and compassion, the Mature Masculine's highest self has made legacy divine, turning it into a pool of fond memories and a source of inspiration for generations to come.

In living his highest ideal, the Mature Masculine represents the wisdom elegantly noted in the *Upanishads* (some of the ancient Indian texts);
"Atmada balada"

[Giving strength (to others) by giving himself].

It is the highest passionate intention of the Mature Masculine to have left behind a noble legacy when he departs his physical existence. This urge does not come from an egoistic need for making use of this world, and seek recognition so that his epitaph may show that he was a man of good deeds. Neither does the urge come from his desire to be posthumously renowned for his great contribution – whatever that may be. His urge comes out of the genuine and pure intention to want to bring fulfilment into the lives of those around - whether it is a simple smile - by bringing to bear that latent gift, that unique blessing that he – and he alone – is endowed with on his visit on earth this lifetime. He seeks to leave the world a better place than it was when he arrived.

* * * * * * * *

In his daily practice of living his mission, transcending life and death, and giving himself up for leaving his noble legacy behind, the Mature Masculine asks himself;

- ✓ When did I last feel the pure joy of giving at the detriment of my inner and material comforts?
- ✓ Will every thought, word or deed of mine today be a future testimonial of the divine within me or the demon within me?

21.RIGHTEOUS ANGER, THE ENERGY THAT RIGHTS THE WRONG

"You destroyed the Cupid,
Thou art the Father
Of Ganesha and Subramanya,
You cut the head of proud Daksha."

(Sarvalinga Stava)

It is 5000 BC and these are turbulent times in India. Aryans, who migrated to India from the northwest have brought their own culture, language and teachings. On the other hand are the indigenous people of the land with their own culture, language and teachings. The Aryans considered the indigenous people less wise in the truths of life. When the indigenous clans were attacked and the men were turned slaves, and the women carried away, Shiva exclaimed, "This is atrocious, this is injustice!". His righteous anger prompted Him to declare that the less strong ones be protected. He urged those capable of safeguarding the less strong from inconsiderate beings. Clans started to unify.

When the caste system originated, different classes of people were defined. With each class came a set of rights. This meant that huge swaths of the indigenous population, including slaves, women and the 'untouchables' were deprived of their right to practice spirituality. Out of Shiva's righteous anger was born His path of spiritual realization, otherwise known as Shaiva Dharma. Shaiva Dharma did not discriminate between peoples. No one was ignored, neither the Aryans, nor the non-Aryans, nor the women, nor the 'untouchables'.

Shiva never got angry at anything that happened to Him, because His ego was never at stake. But He was angered by social injustice. He interceded on behalf of the oppressed and downtrodden, rescuing them from the onslaught of injustice meted out by the merciless.

* * * * * * * *

Righteous anger is an accompaniment of man's inner divinity, and resides even in the character of Shiva. And like a serpent coming out of its sleep, righteous anger rears its head in the presence of social injustice. History is littered with essays of man's ego getting the better of him, leading him to take advantage of humanity and Nature, plundering for his own regard. Over and over again, man has succumbed to the yearnings of his lower self, that self in him that is unyielding and narrow, that reflects no light, that is blind to the Infinite. He has let his sometimes insatiable greed get the better of him, greed that is the illegitimate craving to acquire for himself at the detriment of others. And after the ego has played its dance of self-gratification, and its pride of possession, and its insolent alienation of heart, through sighs of discontent, through the weariness of failure, through the regrets for the past, through the anxieties for the future, has always risen the Mature Masculine's righteous anger. It has righted the wrong, balanced the scales, restored humanity's faith in itself, and returned people into loving, healing relationships. This righteous anger has risen out of the longing of his heart to reveal his higher self, to seek that is common to all, and to meld that is one with all there is and the Infinite.

If the antithesis to what his highest being - his inner divine - truly believes in pervades his or others' lives, the Mature

Masculine rightly feels righteous anger. However, there is a danger to righteous anger. When righteous anger becomes malicious and ungodly, it ceases to be righteous. Such anger must be addressed, and addressed instantly. For anger that is not metabolized coagulates within him, becoming part of his being, driving his habits and reasserting itself repeatedly. It metastasizes as disease in his mind and body, it depletes his vital energy bestowed upon him with a higher purpose, and it degrades his relatedness with himself and all.

Many a man creates and traps his anger in his inner dungeons, as an alien to be castigated, as a cancer to be disowned, until the day it breaks free of its bindings and gate-crashes out of the confines of man's inner self to consume in its fury those around him. In its blinding light, in its fiery heat, like a racing chariot without a charioteer, it tramples all including himself. His mind, soaked in its anger, becomes impaired in its thinking. It sees no reason, and like acid in a metal container, the anger corrodes the container first before scalding others.

"*Krodha eva maha shatru*" [9]
[Anger is a great enemy].
So said Shiva. He meant that anger impedes man's progress towards self-realization. It would have man destroyed should he surrender to it, for anger is nothing but man unconsciously recollecting his inner pain. And when man expresses his anger, it makes him self-obscured and lost, numbs him from feeling himself beyond his personal surroundings, blots out his greater self, pathetically lets his truth remain unrealized. Worst of all, it breeds fear among others. This fear impairs assimilation of thoughts and ideas, drains love from the weeping heart, damages perspective of the true standard of values, breaks the

harmony of our life in every moment, and ruptures the channel of the heart's communication with others and with the Infinite.

Hence the Mature Masculine owns his transformation by mastering that split second between any input that he receives and the output that he shares. By exercising unconsciously skilled awareness upon that moment between input and output, the Mature Masculine is aware of the infinite possibilities that lay within him to consciously create the reaction that he chooses. Any feeling created in man has an inner reference, a reference that has been shaped by lifetimes and lifetimes of experiences. These experiences occupy in man's subconscious a space as vast as the sky, as deep as the ocean. Mapped and measured against these experiences, every input creates a reaction. "Once bitten, twice shy", as the saying goes, every past experience casts a shadow over man's current reactions to inputs. Rather than apportion blame upon those who triggered his anger, the Mature Masculine finds the reasons for his anger in his lifetimes of accumulated experience.

Further, the Mature Masculine ensures that his righteous anger speaks to himself and not to others. As the choice-maker of his own reality, he – and not his anger - determines how he chooses to express his reaction to the event or action that triggered his righteous anger. Becoming the witness of his righteous anger, he attentively listens to the voice of anger and hears its words of knowing. He asks himself, "What is it that needs to be different against which I must register my view?"

He is aware that there is a big difference between him feeling righteous anger and him expressing it. It is in his expression of righteous anger that he is different from the immature souls on earth. The Mature Masculine chooses to become aware of his righteous anger, recognize that the event or action that has triggered his righteous anger goes against his deeply held values. He lets himself feel that anger, recognizing that he has created it and that it is part of his being.

Anger is commonly a sin; righteous anger is often a duty. Righteous anger protects those that seek to surrender into the protection of the Mature Masculine. Righteous anger announces the presence of his, the Mature Masculine. It turns him into a catalyst and propeller for social change. However, no matter how reprehensible the people or activities the Mature Masculine is condemning, he does so with a calm mind, not giving into sin in his responses, and unwinding the cycle of *Samskaras* (the burden of consequences of one's good and bad actions). Even in his righteous anger, he has the infinite capacity to forgive.

*　*　*　*　*　*　*　*

As the Mature Masculine continues on his path of living his fullest, and channels his righteous anger to right the wrong, in order to identify if his anger is righteous in nature or simple self-serving, he asks himself;

- ✓ Do I recognize anger when I am experiencing it within?
- ✓ Is my anger triggered by injustice meted out upon the collective goodness of mankind, or out of a self-serving ideology?
- ✓ Do I let my anger speak to myself as a reminder of my innerpain, or do I channel its energy towards those who triggered it, and hold them responsible for my anger?

22.PROTECTOR: THE SWIFT STRENGTH OF THE MATURE MASCULINE

"He who, though gifted with the power,
to stomach deadly poison, to burn to ashes love
and metamorphose doomsday's fire
to his glowing forehead-eye,

still bears the ambrosial moon,
the mountain daughter and the heavenly stream,
so wondrous is his skill of policy,
may he, Great Shankara, protect you".
(Shubhasita ratna kosha)

Vajra: A kind of powerful weapon invented and used by Shiva. He used this weapon to protect the honest and virtuous people as well as innocent birds and animals, and to strike at the sinful, violent and arrogant anti-social elements. Shiva was very restrained and self-composed in all spheres of life; He would use His weapon only on rare occasions. From a perusal of history we learn that He never used His weapon against any virtuous person. It is believed that human beings as well as animals in trouble used to approach Shiva for security; Shiva would protect them and admonish their enemies to move along the path of righteousness. By repeated persuasion He tried to rectify their defects. Only against those who refused to correct their ways and, on the contrary, tried to further their own self-interest by opposing Shiva, He would use this weapon. Since it was used to promote the welfare of all living beings, it was rightly called 'Shubhavajra' (the thunderbolt of welfare).

(Adopted from Namah Shivaya Shantaya, Shrii Shrii Anandamurti)

*   *   *   *   *   *   *   *

The single greatest epic told and retold, handed down from generation to generation is that of man's sacrifice to protect those beloved to him and the values he cherished most within himself. He has fought until the last breath, laying down his life in the ultimate sacrifice, so that humanity could look at itself in the mirror with dignity. Around campfires men have exchanged and exhorted history of men who stood up to protect, in playgrounds children have fantasized and mimicked the great heroes of their epics and civilizations, in bedtime stories mothers have enflamed the imaginations of their children with the glorious stories of protective kings and princes. The Mature Masculine's mission to protect has been inspired by his undying faith in the undying love within us, his heart's dearest longing for oneness with the Cosmic Consciousness, and whenever he has planted the flag at the peak of his frontiers, it has been his heart realizing its unity in love.

It is in man's instinct to protect, as it was in Shiva's instinct to protect. The instinct to protect his loved ones from harm and his ideals from corrosion lies at the core of mature masculinity, and it is an immensely powerful force. Man's instincts, attitudes and physical strength empower him for tough-minded, sacrificial service to those people who count most in his life. His muscles, his resolve, his endurance, his craftsmanship, his assertiveness, his abstraction gifts of mind, his ability to connect cause and effect, his far-reaching vision, his intellectual power, his strong sense of fairness, his ethical conduct, all endowed as boons to man in his pursuit of the unification of hearts and ideals.

It is the Mature Masculine's mission, the challenge that brings out the best in him, to be the power and provision for the universe to continue its ceaseless cycle of dissolution and renewal. It is also his mission to be the secure fortress for the operative force of *Shakti* (the divine feminine component of the Cosmic Consciousness), a fortress that inspires the feminine heart to nurture herself and others with the bottomless reservoir of love it carries. The Mature Masculine naturally holds as his duty to be the lifelong beacon of integrity and morality to his offspring to expand into a being of dignity and conscience. As the protector, for those around he is the benchmark for how to comport themselves justly and honourably in the world of beings. In his service, he deals with a deep sense of self-knowledge, he exhibits his personal integrity, while deferring to others' rights and feelings.

When confronted by the vain endeavours of those who move in narrow circles of immediate self-interest, the Mature Masculine becomes greater than his limited human self. The higher nature in him which always seeks to transcend its human confinements awakens and expresses itself thereby revealing its true meaning.

This is well noted in the *Upanishads* (some of the ancient Indian texts);
"Swasthi no brihaspati drathatu"
[May the Absolute ensure our welfare.]

When faced with situations that warrant his protection, the Mature Masculine accesses his inner divine that is greater than himself. Like a foghorn blaring through the fog, his righteous anger - that is reserved in its expression but forceful in its intent - blares the reminder of his protective presence to all there is.

And when dark forces of civilization or society rear their heads, the indomitable spirit of man's self rises to assert its full force to send those dark forces back into the indeterminate depths of its origin. He asserts loving leadership, and coordinates all his inner faculties towards a single great purpose in life, protecting the wellbeing of all that means much to him. The pain that he incurs in his act of protection has the detachment of eternity, and its harmony in great love. To reveal his noble intent, he willingly gives up everything he has, his willing sacrifice being its own remuneration.

The Mature Masculine's sacrificing spirit as protector is not a compulsion for him, neither is it an unsolicited necessity thrust upon him, rather a duty which is a noble, self-sacrificing adventure. As long as all that is beloved to him are in his care, he will not quit or slacken in his efforts to serve them with his space of security. He will protect and provide no matter what the cost, for they are the meaning of his life, the object of his manly powers, the centre of his heart.

The Mature Masculine's spirit of protection lies on an even keel. This spirit is finely and firmly woven into his sanely internalized powers of judgment, his acute ethical responsibility, his realistic sense of his strengths and limitations, and his consideration for others. He does not let his pride blind him to truth, and he uses his emotions as a barometer to gauge the essence of his external reality, rather than as the lever for his actions. In his pursuit of righting the wrongs, with his firm sense of protection from the deadly affliction of sin, he combines correction with affectionate forgiveness, understanding, and encouragement.

The Mature Masculine, out of his deep love becomes the provider of a safe shelter for those who rely on him, the provider of stability in chaos, the provider of solidarity in division, the provider of subsistence in scarcity, the provider of warmth in cold, the provider of consolation in grief, the provider of hope in darkness, the provider of meaning in emptiness, the provider of laughter in bleakness, the provider of sociability in fracture, the provider of strength in falter, the provider of comfort in distress, the provider of certainty in indeterminacy, the provider of direction in confusion, the provider of protection in fear, the provider of peace in turbulence, the provider of quiet in anxiety, the provider of passion in inaction, the provider of inspiration in gloom, the provider of firmness in apprehension, the provider of encouragement in dispiritedness, the provider of equanimity in judgment.

* * * * * * * *

In order to live and express his natural protector self, and bring his swift strength to bear upon his world, the Mature Masculine asks himself;

- ✓ Do I stand up for – and defend - the undying love that holds all beings together?
- ✓ Am I driven by my magnanimous heart's yearning to wield its power to protect, or are my actions motivated by fear of survival and self-preservation?
- ✓ Do my beloved and others surrender in my care or when they are in my space?

23.PRINCIPLE-CENTEREDNESS: THE STAIRWAY OF CONSCIOUSNESS

"Appropriateness carries within itself the freedom of choice,
Of being able to say 'yes' or 'no';
Appropriateness carries within itself
the responsibility of acting in harmony with the end purpose;
Appropriateness exudes the concern
for the welfare and happiness of all that are affected by the action;
Appropriateness is the fine application of truth and rationality
to the problems facing us from day to day, whether big or small;
Appropriateness is the way of discriminating,
the task of discerning what is in tune with destiny or Dharma,
with an urge to evolve into one's highest possibility;
Appropriateness is to do what is just right,
at the right time, in the right measure, with the right spirit,
in the right way and for the right effect;
Appropriateness is what shall be ultimately judged right
even when the action has long been forgotten or receded into oblivion
from the public memory;
Appropriateness relates not only to the motivation,
intent or the philosophy underlying each action
but also to the process,
to the methods employed
and to the results and consequences of the action in question;
To act appropriately is indeed to walk on the path of virtue,
on the road of cardinal values."[35]

In the 'Manasa-Mabgala-Kavya', ancient devotional recital of Shiva, it is believed that Manasa Devi, the snake goddess, was born of Shiva. Given her lineage, she sought the devotion of a merchant, who remained devoted only to Shiva. A furious Manasa Devi destroyed all his property, only to be eschewed by the merchant. It is believed that she washed away all his belongings and his fellow-men, leaving him on the brink of death. Yet he did not shift his allegiance from Shiva, for his devotion came from his heart. She tried to seduce the merchant into worshipping her, but his love saw only Shiva in its eyes. Enraged, she killed the merchant's kith and kin, including his sons. Even that did not shake his devotion to Shiva.

As the saga of torture continued, softened by the pleas of his mother and wife, he once indifferently flung a flower at Manasa Devi's image, his heart still with Shiva. In the face of the merchants principle-centeredness, Manasa Devi restored to him all that she had taken away from him.

* * * * * * * *

Principle-centeredness is the bow from which the arrow of every thought, word and deed is launched. It is the redline that passes through every facet of the Mature Masculine's life. Through its consistency, through its predictability, it blends into oneness with him until all rise to recognize his principles as integral to his being. Principles may be divine or demonic, it is not for this text to discriminate them. However, it is worthwhile to recognize that principles are neither instincts nor sentiments.

Instinct is ingrained deeply within man's subconscious and is habitual in nature. Lower forms of animals and birds – especially the egg-laying animals – have an underdeveloped mind, and hence are instinctive in nature. What they need to know for their survival and procreation is inborn in them. Man is born with several survival instincts as well. Nature has bestowed upon him these gifts to ensure his survival and multiplication. His acquired instincts are a product of all of his accumulated experiences and thus it is more a reflection of his past experiences than his principles. If a man has been hurt in the past by a dog, this past experience could become part of his instinct motivating him to stay away from dogs, or mistreat them.

Through rigorous practice, man can cultivate new instincts. As he starts to master the faculties attached to his lower instincts – namely survival and procreation – automatically he starts to develop the instincts of a higher order, thus rendering his lower instincts dormant. For example, self-identity may become his new aspiration, and this aspiration in due time grows into an instinct. For the Mature Masculine, once having mastered his lower instincts, his dormant yearning of welfare, self-awareness and oneness starts surfacing and expressing itself. This is the also the starting point of his spiritual voyage.

Principles are not sentiments. Sentiments are seen alongside instinct in the higher forms of animals, mammals for examples. Mammal mothers exhibit a sentimental bond for their young. This bonding supersedes instinct. Bonding between animals and humans, ideologies grounded in extreme emotions, geo-sentiments, patriotism, religious sentiments, and territorialism are all examples of sentiments.

Though man possesses principles, his highest principles often lie dormant under the debris of his instincts and sentiments. The principle-centred man lives his values, doctrines or tenets developed either through unconscious inculcation of himself, or born out of his conscious discrimination. While man unconsciously inherits values from childhood or is habituated in certain doctrines through cultural programming, consciously acquired values are the sculptures of his intellect. For example, man may have unconsciously acquired from his parents the habit of saving his old possessions, while he may have consciously embodied the principle of serving the underprivileged.

The Mature Masculine uses his sharp intellect to execute his *Viveka* (powers of discrimination). Discrimination is the use of man's intellect to penetrate into the truth of things. This penetration helps the Mature Masculine to see the true nature of every being, animate or inanimate. And once the true nature becomes visible, his most divine inner guidance system tells him which is right and which is wrong, which is harmful and which is enriching, which is good and which is bad. In his stewardship of welfare, Shiva used his superior intellect to raise his cognizance of good and bad. This served him in structuring the foundation of civilization as seen today.

With his powers of discrimination, the Mature Masculine brings to his consciousness those values that he chooses his life to be governed by. Through rigorous practice, his habits are aligned with his values, his actions become congruent with his thoughts and words, and he becomes principle-centred. His principles form the common denominator for every thought and action that he undertakes, and they flow out of his nature effortlessly. His flow in his state of principle-centeredness comes through his rigorous practice of peeling those layers of old habits, and embodying a principle-centred life. Through constant awareness, the Mature Masculine sheds his layers and layers of instinctive and sentimental habits, until the new skin becomes visible and natural to himself. In this process of deconstruction, often he experiences confusion, doubt and discomfort, but the Mature Masculine recognizes that all this pain is the gift bestowed upon him by the Divine.

Pain, which is the feeling of man's finiteness, is not a fixture in his life. It is not an end in itself, as joy is. To meet with pain is to know that it has no part in the true permanence of Creation. Like the wind that carries pollens to their destinations, great teachers appear with their whispers of wisdom in man's life. After planting the seeds of truth in man, these teachers leave as swiftly as they arrive. Similar is the nature of pain, the greatest among the great teachers. It arrives with the intention of preserving and serving man to flourish, it aspires to guide him towards the joy he deserves. Though it shifts restlessly on its feet, always in haste to leave, the nature of physical and emotional pain is such that if man does not pay heed to it, like an unwelcome visitor, it appears again with greater intensity. It remains a frequent visitor at his doorstep until it has delivered its parcel, a parcel containing a valuable lesson of life's journey. Man will embody his lessons of growth depending on his threshold for pain and his awareness for growth. The greater his threshold for pain, the later in life the lesson in store for him is embraced. The later in life the lesson is embraced, the slower his growth to higher consciousness. After his first burn, if the child does not learn to be careful with hot pans, his lessons of safety will become his only through more painful burns.

Rarely would the Mature Masculine inflict pain upon fellow beings, except to admonish those dear to him to bring them on the path of *Dharma* (life's highest purpose), to invite them to shed their veil of darkness, to encourage them to claim lasting peace, love and joy that is intended for them. In his noble act of living his mission to serve others, he is not swayed by concerns of temporary "unpopularity", for all-round welfare is his heart's motivation. Deep within, his highest nature is aware that time will transmute any resentment - which has its origin in man's veil of darkness or the fallacy of the ego - into trust, credibility, attraction, respect, awe, allegiance, commitment to cause.

The Mature Masculine is aware of the role of pain in his life. He recognizes that within him is a part that is immortal, a part that is not intimidated by pain and sufferings, for he sees in pain the treasure of joy. He owns within himself the choice-maker who can turn pain into good account, to transmute it into joy. He seeks not to be deprived of his right to face his pain, for in pain is symbolized the infinite possibility of perfection, the pathway to his wisdom, his love, his eternal joy.

Whatever principles man may have, to identify them and live by them is alignment. Through every event and every experience that man is part of, he is being constantly tested for his alignment with his principles. Either aware or unaware, he is responding to these tests. His conscious response, though, brings greater self-realization within himself unlike a purely mechanical engagement with every event and experience. This greater self-realization reinforces his higher ideals, enlivens his inner divine, and propels him further on his journey towards the Infinite.

Man flourishes when his principles and practice enjoin together. Decline begins when his practice is in conflict with his principle. This is true for the individual as well as the collective. Civilizations, long known for their lode of wisdom, have vanished when they have lost their connectedness to their source. Interpretations get in the way, egoism snares its teeth, practice diverges with principles, and before you know, man has fallen from his pedestal.

As is said in the *Upanishads* (some of the ancient sacred texts):
"Ichavasyamidam sarvam yat kincha jagatyan jagat"
[We are enjoined to see whatever there is in the world as being enveloped by the Infinite.]
Thus it is the Mature Masculine's endeavour to always shine his inner godliness through his daily perseverance to constantly align his practice with his principles. That is his daily spiritual practice of principle-centeredness; realizing and affirming the presence of the Infinite within himself.

* * * * * * * *

In his daily practice of re-enforcing his principle-centeredness, the Mature Masculine constantly self-reflects on the following questions;

- ✓ Am I unshakably consistent in what I believe in, even under repeated and rigorous pressure?
- ✓ The forces that propel me through life, are they instincts, sentiments or principles?
- ✓ What is the lesson that my pain is trying to teach me?
- ✓ Does temporary unpopularity discourage me from standing up for the long-term welfare of those dear to me?

24.SELF-RESTRAINT: TRANSCENDING HIS HUMAN LIMITS

"Uttam Sanyam Dharma"
[Supreme self-restraint is innate]
(Upanishads)

In real life as well as in Indian mythology, the love of Parvati, the daughter of Himalaya, the mountain king, towards Shiva is a saga of singular dedication and beauty. She undertakes the severest of penances to win the hand of the ascetic of Kailash, Shiva, and wins in the end.

As a maiden, Parvati chose to serve Shiva in his practice of austerities, and as an ascetic He restrained any necessity for a woman's service. Parvati countered, "The power of cognition (known as the masculine core) cannot exist without the force of manifestation (known as the feminine core). So why do You deny my presence?" Impressed by Her resolve, Shiva let Her serve His practice.

As the gods connived to create attraction in Shiva for Parvati, He resisted their attempts by immolating the god of love with His third eye, the eye of fire. An inconsolable but resolute Parvati cast off the luxuries of Her parents, Her fine clothes and jewellery to spend a life of a hermit in the wilderness. She slept on the crude cold ground, barely ate a grain, and spent Her life in penance and thought of Shiva. After sustained devotion, She broke through His restraint and won His heart.

* * * * * * * *

Though self-restraint is deeply embedded and embodied in the essence of the following two chapters, this chapter will treat this subject apart and ahead. This so because in itself self-restraint is one of the most spiritually growth-enhancing *Sadhana* (spiritual practice) that propels man forward in his embodiment of the mature masculinity.

It is appropriate to ask, "why self-restraint?"
Self-restraint because it is every beings' highest purpose to pursue *Brahma*, the Supreme Consciousness. *Brahma* resides within all beings. Not by looking for it elsewhere, rather man must seek it through his practice of restful awareness and contemplation, through meditation, through *seva* (selfless service), and ultimately through self-realization. None of this can be achieved without restraint of both the sensorial urges and ego-driven propensities of the human mind.

While the appreciation and acknowledgment of the splendours of creation is self-restraint, lecherous gratification of man's senses is self-indulgence. While fulfilling his hunger is self-restraint, gluttony is self-indulgence. This discusses how he must practice self-restraint with his sensorial urges.

Many of the propensities of the mind are positive in nature. While propensities like repentance, aspiration for noble actions, sweet expressions, spiritual longing, etc. are the positive propensities of the mind, there are a number of ego-driven propensities of the mind. The experience originating from the ego-driven propensities of the mind are as fleeting in nature, as the propensity itself. They distract man from the unending experience of bliss that is the Creation's commandment for all.

Some of the ego-driven propensities (*vrittis* in Sanskrit) are vanity, mine-ness mentality, hypocrisy, anxiety, envy, fear, hatred, indulgence, lack of confidence, psychic stupor, belittlement of others, sadistic tendencies, lethargy, yearning for possession, argumentativeness, repulsive expression, etc. Self-restraint is the exercising of man's will as a way of overcoming the urges of the ego.

Though man is superior than a brute, he can sink even lower than a brute. It is all a matter of choice. He who can distinguish the perishable nature of the flesh from the imperishable nature of the spirit instinctively knows that self-realization is impossible without self-discipline and self-restraint. The body may either be a playground of unbridled desires, or a temple of self-realization. The Mature Masculine recognizes that the propensities of the mind are all fleeting in nature, as are his sensorial urges. It is as with the case of smoking, the real physiological urge for smoking stays for a few minutes when it is 'smoking time' – like after a meal – and whether catered to or not, will soon disappear thereafter. Thus for the Mature Masculine, self-restraint is the mastery of the fluttering of the mind.

The greater the capacity to restrain himself, the greater also is the power man feels within his own self. We have heard that there is a variety of powers in this world. There is monetary power, muscular power, political power, social power, intellectual power, etc., but these are all external to the wielder of the power. In some cases they are only foisted upon a person. The powers of Shiva are not adjectives to his existence. They are not his qualifications. They are his very presence. He is the benchmark for the Mature Masculine in his pursuit of eternal bliss through oneness with all.

Self-restraint is itself a power because all the avenues of depletion of energy are rerouted into the very existence of the saint or the seeker or the sage. The channels through which energy moves outward in the direction of things and objects in the world get melted down into the menstruum of self-control. Things become the very subject, the very meditator, the contemplator, the beholder, the visualizer of themselves. In this unity, the Mature Masculine can feel his immense power that comes from his self-restraint. It radiates abundantly out of him filling him with the experience of passion and joy as he continues purposefully on his *Dharma* (reason for existence).

Self-restraint is exercising man's restrain over the expression of the illegitimate component of his emotions like anger or hysteria. The illegitimate component of man's emotions is the penumbra of his feelings. The emotions are there, however they are a spill over of the shadow created by his own mental makeup. This illegitimate component is not directed towards any 'perpetrator' in particular, rather its locus is internal in nature. Through man's *Samskaras* (the burden of consequences of one's good and bad actions) and his upbringing, he has given birth to those emotions. The presence of these emotions is not the *carte blanche* for man to vent them towards the ones who trigger those sensations within him, rather they are an invitation for him to go into himself to heal the wounds from which these fountains of emotions gush. It takes the Mature Masculine the practice of self-restraint to turn his flashlight of discrimination inwards on those *Samskaras* (the burden of consequences of one's good and bad actions) within.

Man must learn to give space for the subtle over the gross. Humanity is used to rush to the catharsis of every event presenting itself upon him. If man is watching a movie, he is restless to know the end. If he is in the act of sexual intimacy, he wants to reach the orgasm. If he is cooking, his mind gets set on the eventual taste of the dish. Subtlety is the expression of the inner feminine. To let the inner feminine express itself in all its subtleties, man must moderate his inner adolescence. By doing so, he creates intimate contact with every moment, every sensation, and every thought that passes through him. The Mature Masculine recognizes that every moment has a meaning, and to experience that meaning is Nature's will. He uses his inner feminine as a scoop to dig into and uncover the meaning of each moment. The self-restraint he employs upon his inner adolescence gives space to the expression of the inner feminine to unfold the endless moment to moment joy of 'being'.

Like everything else that brings good in life, self-restraint too requires an inexhaustible store of patience. There is absolutely no reason to despond, and there must be no brooding over man's failure at self-restraint. And there should be no conscious effort to drive away unpleasant thoughts. Such efforts will also constitute a form of indulgence, an overdose of ideology. The best prescription is non-resistance, that is, accepting the existence of unpleasant thoughts, and giving space to those thoughts to play out their acts, lose their energy and - like hurricanes losing their steam after a while – disappear in ether.

Self-restraint can be misunderstood. I once heard a story that well underlines the essence of self-restraint. There was once a spiritual teacher who was a practicing vegetarian. One day a visitor brought some fresh patties as a gift to the teacher and his disciples. As the teacher graciously accepted the gift with a smile, one of the disciples asked the visitor, "Are these patties vegetarian?" With a look of shock and guilt, the visitor replied apologetically, "No! In my excitement of meeting you, I completely forgot that you were practicing vegetarians." As she stood there with a guilty look on her face, the teacher casually opened the gift and joyously consumed a patty.

While the teacher was a vegetarian, he was not a victim of his ideology to the extent of dishonouring the pure and noble intention of the visitor. Self-restraint thus is not just man living in alignment with his principles or ideology, it is also being free from condemning those who do not align with his ideology.

* * * * * * * *

As the Mature Masculine continues with his daily practice of self-restraint in order to transcend his human limits to access that which is divine within him, he asks himself;

- ✓ As I continue on my path of self-realization, can I transcend my sensorial urges and the propensities of my mind in order to postpone gratification?
- ✓ Am I choosing for the immense power of self-restraint, over the indulgence and extravaganze of my ego?
- ✓ Can I direct my attention and energy to this moment, and experience the meaning of the moment, instead of rushing to the climax of my experience?

25.RADIATING HIS LIGHT OF RENUNCIATION

"Om Trayambakam Yajaamahé
Suganghim Pushtivardhanam
Urvaarukmiva Bandhanaan
Mrityor Mokshiya Mamritaat"
[I worship thee, O' sweet Lord of transcendental vision.
O' giver of prosperity to all,
may I be free from the bonds of death,
even as a melon is severed from its bondage or attachment to the creeper.]
(Maha Mrityunjay Mantra)

Shiva is also known as 'Trilochana', the Three-eyed One, in the centre of whose forehead is the 'Gnana-chakshu' (the third eye), the eye of wisdom. The burning power of the wisdom of the third eye destroys desires for worldly objects. Sensual desire and lust is represented by 'Kamadev', the god of love and carnal passion. When a person reaches a state of perfect renunciation, he is said to have burnt all his desires. Shiva's third eye burnt to ashes 'Kamadev'. The flames shooting from the third eye incinerating the god of carnal passion is the metaphor for mastering desires. This incineration is the image of dissolving the ego's drives for excesses. The eye of wisdom leads to transcendental vision of the Supreme Reality.

Different traditions of Shiva's followers have existed for millennia, and each school practices the principles of renunciation in widely varying ways. Cults exist who endeavour assiduously with the help of the yoga of monasticism to master their desires and become pure in mind. They overcome the desire for offspring, the desire for wealth, the desire for worlds, and they live the life of a mendicant.

Then there are schools which practice renunciation through freeing themselves from their perceived delusion of monastic rituals and attachment, choosing instead to access alternate realities of mind through shamanistic practices, negating prevailing social life and social behaviour. Their beliefs and daily practices are tuned to actively soliciting social censure, in order to achieve isolation from the worldly existence.

Then there are those devotees of Shiva who practice renunciation through the experience of excesses. They splurge themselves into intoxication, fish, flesh, sexual activity and parched grain, through which they aim to master avarices of the mind and ego.

Different beliefs, different paths, but common destination.

* * * * * * * *

Man, with his worldly needs - needs of the nature of clothing, housing, food, companionship, etc. - has a legitimate duty to provide for himself and his beloved who rely on him for their healthy and safe subsistence. While he must resolutely and sincerely pursue such legitimate needs, it is his prerogative to simultaneously maintain a synergistic relationship with all beings of Creation.

While needs are themselves an integral part of modern man's existence, his relationship with his needs matter more than the needs themselves. Desire is his victim hood to needs, the expressions of his ego, legitimate or illegitimate, that awaken to periodically remind him of his limitedness that comes with his human existence. Desire, always with its face turned towards results, is that hungry brute that once fulfilled, goes into slumber under the shade of its own satiation, only to wake up soon to exert its existential will over man again. It exerts upon man in a repeating cycle, thus seeking to magnify its existence through repeated demands for more. This truth is elegantly captured in the following verse from the *Upanishads* (some of the ancient Indian texts);

"Ya hy eva putraisana sa vittaisana ya vittaisana sa lokaisana, ubhé hy eté esané eva bhavatah"
[That which is the desire for sons is the desire for wealth; that which is the desire for wealth is the desire for the worlds, for both these are but desires.]

Desire is not specific, it specifies not a particular need, and like a child in a toy store screaming for his favourite toy, desire's cry of yearning gets louder when it comes in the presence of that which appeals to man's ego. It carries not a reference external to man, its only reference being the ego, internal to man. Man who acquires the object of his desire, puts his desire to sleep for a while, until it rears its head again, screaming for something anew. And so the perpetual cycle continues, from wakefulness to sleep and back, from life to death and back, over and over.

It is only a naïve man who believes that he can forever quench desires through fulfilling his needs. He lives in the fervent hope that one day he can resurrect himself from his victim hood of his desire, the voice that is very own to him never expressing itself, but like a pet drawn by the noose around its neck, shall he be carried through life by his desires. The Mature Masculine owns the knowing that desire resides within himself, that how hard he may try to appease it, that how benevolently he may satiate his desires with external objects, his liberation from the bondage of desire lies within. Hence he focuses unto himself, looking to find within himself the roots of his desire, recognizing the affliction of his ego. He refrains from fertilizing his desires through satiating it each and every time, instead refusing his ego of its nutrients, refusing to indulge his desires, refusing to pamper his ego, to be free to be led by his highest will, that noble inner spirit that is none other than the Shiva within, who in his form as '*Kamantakari*' is known as the destroyer of desires.

Man's modern day life is a drumbeat of acquisitions. He runs from pillar to post, driven by his will to acquire. To acquire, he will leave no stones unturned, he will leave no resource untouched, and he will hesitate not in the process to disrupt the delicate balance of Nature. Man is the only being on earth that is capable of using freewill to carve his own ways, ways different from the will of Nature. Other beings have their pursuits inborn into their instincts. Their instincts keep them on their path, and take them directly to their destinies. In order to support It maintain Its delicate balance, Nature has bestowed upon man a superior intellect. However, in his thirst for acquisition, the very intellect that has been Nature's gift to him, he uses with no hesitation to disrupt the delicate balance of Nature.

The Mature Masculine on the other hand, relinquishes force, aligns himself with the will of Nature, and uses his pure and passionate intention to attract towards him that what he deserves. He manifests through his immense power of attraction, remaining detached from his intentions, giving space to his intentions to blossom and manifest on their own. He renounces his drive to acquire, and opens himself towards the abundance reserved for him, allowing himself to surrender into the flow of Nature, attracting forth dispassionately only that which is essential to him. This immense power of attraction that the Mature Masculine possesses is best embodied by the following passage;

"Attraction is the underlying theme in the play of this creation.
Desires, urges, passions and longings-
All carry the force of attraction
To the Infinite One.

Just as iron particles are attracted by the magnet;
Just as the bee is irresistibly drawn by the pollen;
Just as sperm rushes to unite with the egg;
Just as the meteor rages towards the earth;

Just as the tides are pulled by the moon;
Just as we draw in the sweet breath to live;
Just as the child yearns to suckle the mother's breast....
So are we dancing to melodies of our deepest longings.

At best, these longings produce masterpieces of creative genius.
At worst, they produce havoc in our world of emotions.
They must, therefore, be handled with caution and care,
with skill and compassion, with wisdom and diligence." [35]

Man has become a polarized being, creating overpowering interpretations of events around him and his pursuits. He is tuned to unconsciously run away from pain and gravitate towards pleasure. He is used to crave for that which he likes, and to feel aversion for that which he does not. He has created his own language for events and pursuits, and this language has imprisoned him into a pattern of feelings that control his reality. He has learned to call sunny weather great weather, and cloudy and rainy weather as lousy weather. He dances and exalts when it is sunny and warm, and inversely he feels helplessly drawn into depression when it is clouded and raining. His polarized craving and aversion has victimized his biology, his mind and body responding with maladies, unlike the centred man who holds within him a reservoir of immense healing.

It is the prerogative of the Mature Masculine to renounce his polarity of judgment, not being elated by successes or deterred by failures – his or others', living his love in action, exhibiting his fellowship in suffering, witnessing with equanimity others' deeds, and recognizing others' actions as originating from their aspirations to self-perfection. The Mature Masculine never takes to heart the evil acts of another, nor does he listen to what is said in dispraise of others. He speaks no evil of another, for he is pure in his heart of all faults, so is he in speech. And when anything is said in dispraise of him, the Mature Masculine witnesses it in silence, compassion and equanimity, for he is aware that the dispraise is an indication of the judgmental nature of the other, than a reflection of his own virtues.

He that humanity knows as the Mature Masculine is never enthralled when honoured and never angry when insulted, and he has given assurances of compassion unto all beings. The Mature Masculine, in his observance of life, does not view death with sorrow, nor does he view life with attachment, he remains wedded to the present.

As the Mature Masculine has no foes, no fear assails him. He who fears no beings and whom no beings fear, can have no fear from any quarter. There from comes forth his observance of the duty of harmlessness, included within that of every other duty. He lives an everlasting life of felicity who avoids injuring other beings, casting an equal eye upon all beings, who is devoted to truth, who is lined with fortitude, who has his senses under control, and who grants protection to all beings. Fear of death succeeds not in overcoming the Mature Masculine who is content with self-knowledge, and who is renounced of desire and expectancy.

He who is known as the Mature Masculine is free from attachments of every kind, lives like space, which while containing everything is yet unattached to anything, who has everything but calls nothing his own, and is tranquil in his soul. Humanity knows him as Mature Masculine who never exerts himself for doing such acts as are done by worldly men, who never bends his head unto any one, or who never insincerely flatters another. All beings are pleased with happiness and filled with fear at the prospect of grief. The Mature Masculine, therefore, who should feel distressed at the prospect of filling other beings with grief, abstains entirely from acts of cruelty and violence.

* * * * * * * *

As the Mature Masculine endeavours to live his worldly life from a place of self-mastery, radiating his light of renunciation in his relationship with everything material, he asks himself daily;

- ✓ What is the nature of my relationship with my needs? Am I a victim of my needs, or do I relate to my needs from a place of self-mastery?
- ✓ Can I renounce my drive to acquire things, and open myself to attract abundance naturally into my life?
- ✓ Do I carry extreme polarities in my reasoning, judgment and emotions?
- ✓ How much do I rely on my own innervoice, and how much do I rely on others' judgments and opinions for my inner well-being?

26.HE INVOKING HIS ASCETIC SELF

"Na mrityur na shanka na jatibhedah
Pita naibo main naibo mata na janma
Na bandhurna mitrang gururnaibo shishyah,
Sachchidanandarupa Shivoham Shivoham

Na punyang na papang na shaukhyang na dukhang
Na mantro na tirtha na vedah na yagah
Ahang bhojanang naibo bhojyang na bhokta
Chidanandarupah Shivoham Shivoham"

[I am beyond death, I am beyond doubts, I am beyond divisions.
No one is my father, none my mother, nor was I born
Neither brother nor friend, neither teacher nor pupil,
I am only truth, ecstasy and consciousness, I am Shiva, I am Shiva.

Nothing is sin for me, nothing is holy, sadness and happiness are not known to me
I do not need chanting, nor holy places, no sacred texts, no rituals
I am neither food, nor do I eat nor am I the enjoyer of these
My abode is always a conscious happiness. I am Shiva, I am Shiva.]
(Devotional song of Shiva)

Shiva, in His form as 'Avadhut' (the ascetic) is the archetype of the serene ascetic, body covered with ashes, sitting deep in meditation on top of Mount Kailash in the Himalayas. As the god of the yogis, Shiva is self-controlled, He is the embodiment of complete peace and quiet. He finds bliss in His self and meets all needs from within, free from His external environment and worldly life. Shiva is often depicted in a meditating posture. His eyes are half-shut to the world, suggesting that at the same time, He is in the world and of it. He is depicted as wearing wild animals' skins, emblematic of His primal energy. His oneness with His breathing, inward and outward flow, is equated with resolving the duality of the ego and the soul, night and day, subject and object, creation and dissolution, light and darkness. He exists in that space without frontiers, that eternal state where He is awake and asleep at the same time.

The ideal that Shiva sought to realize for Himself and for all, led Him often to the isolation of a contemplative life, away from His worldly role as a householder for His dependents, husband for His consorts, and father for His children. Through His asceticism, He penetrated into the mysteries of reality to become one with 'Parama Purusha' (Supreme Consciousness), attaining oneness with the Supreme, becoming all-knowing, and being in perfect harmony with all beings, for He is the form of 'Avadhut'.

* * * * * * * *

He who we know as an ascetic is he who clothes himself with whatever comes by his way, who subsists upon whatever he gets, and who sleeps on whatever spot he finds. He is one who takes time from company, refrains from the full measure of sexual addiction and gratification from eating, for it is only through self-restraint and asceticism that man can access his fullest power and escape the noose of *Karma* (past good or bad actions leading to one's current experiences of joy or sorrow).

On the other hand, man's sensorial bonds only draw him deeper and deeper into the worldly realm of action, each action being the source of renewed experiences and impressions that further reinforce his sensorial urges. And as he progressively gets caught in the trap of his worldly life, he finds himself limited in the manifestation of his fullest potential. He unconsciously marches on to the constant drumbeats of the hectic life around him, as his stream of incessant thoughts continues its cacophony on and on. And like an overloaded processor, he has slowed down in cue with the pacing up of the cacophony. Amidst the din, he performs idly through life, drained out of all his energy, waiting for the next recess in life, dreaming of his next escape before he can regenerate his batteries and reinvent his purposefulness. Life turns into a hamster wheel.

In asceticism there is an eruption of energy, an eruption that acts like a stretched elastic band. Man's practice of asceticism draws him back into his worldly life with renewed vigour, enhanced lustre, greater purposefulness, and a radiant presence – very like Shiva's - that makes his sovereign presence stand in perfection on its own. It is said of Shiva;

"Antah-shariré jyotir-mayo hi shubro yam pashyanti yatayah Kshinadoshah"
[The Supreme Consciousness beholds the ascetics who have done away with their imperfections.]

To access that inner source of his energy, to open that container within and set that energy free, that is the Mature Masculine's path of asceticism, the journey to reconnect with his own inner self through his disconnect with his outer world. His mind must come around to look inwards, through conquering that moment which is controlled by his mind's sensual propensities. And when he has achieved that in the shade of his asceticism, it is akin to hitting the reset button, and awakening that newness which is nature to him.

Man's practice of asceticism erupts that energy within him that is masculine, the energy which creates the cosmic dance between him and the feminine. His masculine energy, human at the same time divine, primal at the same time channelled, relates to his worldly surroundings with polarity, this polarity being that which unconsciously recognizes and relates to the feminine within all. It is the polarizing presence of the mature masculine, the Shiva within man, and the mature feminine, the *Shakti* within woman, which creates the energetic space where Nature unfolds creation, shaping harmony at every step through its union of the contemplation and the action, the cognition and the operation, the intention and the manifestation. This is the ancient truth of the *Purusha* (Cognitive Force) and the *Prakriti* (Operating Force), the masculine and the feminine principles, that manifest and fuel all there is in the universe. In the absence of this energetic space, the process of reinvention and renewal stagnates, the cycle of creation and dissolution comes to a gradual halt, decay and decomposition happens, and extinction follows. All units – visible or invisible – that which exists in this universe, be it the planetary system, union of families, Nature, the chemistry of life and death, or seasons, will be thrown off balance.

Man who has accessed his ascetic side, brings upon himself and others, powers that are abundantly resident within him, his mature masculine force. Being connected to the cosmos, being in union with the All, the Mature Masculine holds in truth his role, for his role is solely in service and welfare, that when he holds the reservoir for masculinity, the feminine essence lives and flourishes alongside. Just as a bird cannot fly without both its wings, the Mature Masculine knows that Nature's wheel of expression cannot rotate in the absence of either force. Thus his ascetic practice becomes his *Dharma* – his duty – to bring forth and live his fullest masculine expression, for then shall the feminine automatically centre around her mature femininity.

When man is absorbed in his physical existence, he is in experience with the worldly reality. All distinctions between the inner and the outer appear, there exists subject and object, there exists discrimination between self and not-self, there exists distinction between ego and non-ego. His truth is material and destructible, his mind is in interaction with the worldly reality, and his body at any moment can fall ill, at any moment can succumb to old age and death. Like a light show in the night sky, like waves on the surface of the ocean, the vastness of life becomes narrowed and impermanent to its aspects of appearing and disappearing. This is what is meant when it is stated in the *Upanishads* (some of the ancient Indian texts);

"Prano mrityuh"
[It is life that is death.]

Man must know with absolute certainty that essentially he is spirit. His true nature is imperishable and eternal. For then, through his practice of asceticism, the Mature Masculine wins mastery over self, by knowing that worldly losses and physical death can take nothing away from the truth and the greatness of his soul, that he can live his truest joy when he has mastered death before he is dead.

It is really courting death when man refuses to accept death, or when he accepts with resignation the finality of death. If man would live with his awareness constantly upon the fact of death, life would seem like a walk on a dirt path in the darkness of night, filled with anxiety at each step taken, in constant effortful attention. Man must simply accept death, neither embracing death like an overshadowing spirit of every act of life and every moment of living, populating the thought of death in every cell of the brain and every corner of the mind; nor rejecting the role of death from the folds of his existential reality, denying its essential role in Nature's act of renewal and elevation, for death is but the antithesis of life. Treated in isolation, death may seem dark and depressing, but when man sees the truth of its integrality with the wholeness of life, he recognizes that death is not ultimate. As that side of the coin that is life expressing its glory and purpose, so is the other side death expressing its release and renewal. The coin finds its wholeness in the inseparability of both its sides, thus death and life finds its harmony in their complementarities. The Mature Masculine looks at life as a child; it as a whole never takes death seriously, rather it laughs, dances and plays, it builds, hoards and loves in death's face. To the child, death is the equivalent of a fall, only to be frowned upon, brushing off the dust and the memory at every fall, to live in liveliness again. This is the knowingness that dawns upon the Mature Masculine through his practice of asceticism.

Inspired to lead the way, the Mature Masculine subjects himself to asceticism in its fullest essence of austerity and solitude, as Shiva did before him, for the Mature Masculine is aware that the practice of austerity and solitude has the same effect as sandpaper on a wooden surface; the more and more the surface is polished, the brighter the shine the surface acquires. With that truth in mind, the Mature Masculine constantly replenishes and recharges the oil lamp of his inner lighthouse with fresh oil, not because his purpose is to burn oil, but to nourish and express his vitality and vigour, his passion and purpose for meaning and growth ever glowing.

Austerity lends to man's training in spiritual life. It cleanses the soul of man, to free it of all that is imperfect about him, and it expands within man all that is noble. Modern man leads an outward life, his soul remains open outwards into the appearance of things. To have a glimpse of the truth he must turn his gaze inwards, and he must bring about an inversion of the natural orientation of his awareness. This he can achieve through wearing down the body through the privation of food and drinks, sleep and comfort, and exposure to heat, cold, rain and wind. Then intake of impressions reduces, the sights he receives through his eyes are far fewer, the sounds that he gathers through his ears are limited, the notes and the impressions that permeate his being through all his senses are lower and less stimulating. With his greater control of his senses thus acquired, the aged soul, ripe for its fullest expression, withdraws his attention from the world, turning his eyes inwards, seeing the soul, for spiritual search has an inward movement leading to the revelation of the divine in the innermost of man.

"Tapasa prapyaté sattvam, sattvat samprapyaté manah
Manasah prapyaté y atma, yam aptva na nivartata iti"
[By austerity goodness is obtained, and from goodness understanding is reached, and from the understanding is the self obtained, and he who obtains the self does not return.]

So it is said of Shiva and his devotees. Stories are told of saints undergoing years of austerities to attain superpowers, and gods having endured austerities in order to create. When man melds his principles and personality, his godliness appears, for that which man calls god, that which is divine about him, resides within. This union between principle and personality he achieves through his judicious practice of austerity, thus letting his mature masculine radiate, illuminating with love and joy his very existence and the lives of those close to him.

Man has often pondered the reason for putting the body and mind through the suffering of asceticism. The simple man has been instructed such, for in it he has been taught will he find his *Moksha*, salvation. It is not for the sake of creating suffering that suffering must be induced in man's life. Suffering, if any, is the by-product of another goal; this goal being to focus the faculties of the mind on self-awareness, and consequently liberation.

Every thought, whether triggered by an external impetus or from an inner recollection, is distracting the mind from its *Dharma*, its innate nature, of expanding awareness in man. In order to focus the faculties of the mind, man must rigorously pursue silence within and around himself, for every impression gathered by the mind leads to a cascade of thoughts and recollections, and every input to the mind leads to some form of assimilation. Every assimilation leads to a reaction of the mind, an output. In short, every impression leads to the constant use of the faculties of the mind. And the constant use of the faculties of the mind drains the mind of its energy to drill into the deeper realms of man's consciousness, identify penetrating truths relevant to his life, create greater awareness for himself, enhance self-knowledge, and unlock the infinite potential that he is gifted with. Unlocking that potential is his challenge.

He must turn away from the world of noise into the inward stillness, the inner silence, to become aware of the ultimate truth which transcends time and space. Create silence, bring men to silence, lest man should not hear the gentle all-knowing word of the Inner Self.

So it is said of Shiva's pursuit of tranquillity in the texts;

"Ekam rupam bahudha yah karoti tam atmastham ye anupachyanti dihrah, tesham sukham chachvatam netaresham." [Only he of tranquil minds, and none else, can attain abiding joy by realizing within his soul the Being who manifests one essence in a multiplicity of forms.]

External solitude leads man to inner solitude, which in turn takes him into the space between thoughts, were the 'I' resides. It is that 'I' which is all-knowing, infinite in its capacity to conceive and materialize, to lead and love. Thus solitude becomes the elixir to man, dousing him in that which is his constant duty to pursue, turning him into the gift unto himself and humanity. Man, who can withdraw his senses and the mind, and consequently make a spot teeming with thousands appear to himself perfectly solitary, he is regarded a Mature Masculine. This he becomes through his rigorous asceticism, making that space for himself where not he is in silence, but becomes of it.

There is solitude everywhere, and man is in truth solitary always. His pursuit is to find it out within, not to seek it outside himself. Solitude is in the mind of man. Man who might be in the thick of the world and maintain serenity of mind, he is one in solitude. Another may abstain from civilization, staying in the forest, but still be unable to control his mind, with no solitude within. Thus solitude is a function of the mind. A man attached to desires can find no solitude within wherever he may be, whereas he who is in detachment is always in solitude. Man might be engaged in worldly life and be free from desire and live in solitude. Man who performs his actions in this manner in every facet of life, he is advanced in asceticism, he is steeped in his mature masculinity.

* * * * * * * *

In his daily practice of owning the full power of asceticism, the Mature Masculine asks himself the following questions;

- ✓ Do I withdraw from my worldly life often enough to be drawn back into it with renewed vigor and greater purposefulness?
- ✓ Do I withdraw frequently enough from my worldly reality to experience charged passion with the feminine?
- ✓ How can I set myself free from the fear of death, knowing that death is only a temporary step in the process of life?
- ✓ How do I seamlessly weave the practice of austerity and solitude into my worldly life, so that I can constantly embody the fullest luster and radiant presence of the Mature Masculine?

27.STABILITY AND FORBEARANCE, HIS UNSHAKEABLE ESSENCE

"It's difficult to be small,
Not difficult to be great!
Not difficult to be a devotee.
It's difficult to be a sign, though not
To be the Tranquil One,
O Chenna Mallikarjuna Lord!"
(Mahadeviyakka, South Indian poetess)

"In mythology it is said of Shiva that He became 'Sthanu', a motionless pillar, a branchless trunk. 'Sthanu', a post, is Shiva's concrete symbol. Its upward direction shows His inflexible stance across the universe, as well as suggesting the forbearance of His mental propensities. The visual concept of 'Sthanu' is the paradoxical negation of sexual excess. The whole of the ascetic Shiva's being is contained within its pillar shape. This abstract pillar shape stands firm by the tension of the implied procreative force, its mastery, and negation.

The motionless pillar is Shiva, the ascetic, in whom the fire of life burns upward inwardly while He stands still. This is the mystery of 'Sthanu'. He is motionless, like a log in which the potentiality of fire is latent and controlled. 'Sthanu' is Shiva the yogi, an aeviternal, immovable presence, pillar of the world. The Mahabharata – one of the Indian epics – sees 'Sthanu' as the origin of life. Its dual significance comprises the irreducible nature of Shiva, the Fire, the origin of life, and Shiva, the Great Yogi, who, counter to nature, is master of the unspent life-giving power."

(Adopted from The Presence of Siva, S Kramrisch)

* * * * * * * *

The protective and affectionate presence of the Mature Masculine exhibits itself in the stability and forbearance that he offers. He portrays stability and forbearance, being (not acting) the solid rock, knowing that all that is external to him – Nature's beings - is transient and fluctuating. Seasons come and go, day fades into night and is reborn, weather keeps changing, and people's thoughts, words and deeds are in perpetual movement. He lets not these fluctuations be mimicked by his internal self, through non-judgment and equanimity he preserves that which is constant within him, his true self.

Neither does he let his true self, his soul, be swayed by his egoic yearnings for prestige, power, recognition, possessions or belongingness. He is not limited in his relatedness with others through the egoic feelings of inferiority, or superiority, or defeatism, or complexes of hopelessness and despair. Complexes, which by their very nature are partial, are not the nature of the soul, as the soul sees no hierarchy. And where there is no hierarchy, man finds no ripples upon the equanimity of his mind.

It is a truly developed man's gift to the world to be the pillar of spiritual stability. Stability is the Mature Masculine's ability to maintain clear, stable attention throughout the practice of life. His quality of discernment allows him to make distinctions between phenomena, and to understand things as they actually are. In his daily path of self-cultivation, he lets go of notions, the product of judgment, to become unshakeable.

His simple-hearted nature lends to his spiritual stability, for he who is simple-hearted does not walk in the counsel of the wicked, nor stand in the company of the impure, nor sit in the seat of scoffers. He holds his mind in clarity through his meditation and restful awareness. He lives in delight, as a tree firmly planted in the law of the Nature, and his principle-centred self knows and trusts his values.

He who we know as the Mature Masculine radiates the symbol of forbearance. He is able to endure and maintain his calm and clarity of intention in the face of obstacles such as delays, adversities and unpleasant sensations. He has the ability to remain in inner peace, being the observer and not a victim when other's seek to create hurt or cause difficulties for him. When misbehaved to, any man with strong moral discipline does not retaliate, but might become angry and restrain the expression of the anger. The Mature Masculine - with his strong forbearance – does not become angry in the first place, for he recognizes that any ill-behaviour from the other is a reflection of the intentions, judgments and impurity of mind of the other, than a reflection of his own nature or behaviour.

That is what is portrayed of Shiva, when it is so said in the ancient texts;
"Na muhyaté, na bhidyaté, na dhayaté, na chidyaté, na kampaté, na kupyaté"
[He is not bewildered, he is not broken, he is not burnt, he is not cut asunder, he does not tremble, he is not angry.]

The mature masculine is aware that to cling on to the pleasant sensation of any moment is to pass his existence living on a swing. A swing that swings forward is preordained to swing backward, that is the unstoppable and undeniable law of Nature. He who fights to hold on to the experience of the moment gone by, for his joy depends on it, lives in negation of that which is truly immanent to him, his soul, whose nature of fulfilment is constant and endless. This is the truth recognized by the Mature Masculine, that his stability and forbearance comes from his freedom from the pleasure of past moments. He who holds on to the experience of any moment finds himself left behind in the past, the lifeline of his existence remaining bound to a past memory. And when that lifeline is severed, his emotions will swing back from the high to the low. Hence, it is the imperative of the Mature Masculine to remain the grateful but equanimous observer of his joyous past. Thus all his inner conflicts and fluctuations are reconciled, and awareness and love is harmonized. It is then that the Formless appears through him as a strong unswayable force in the life of his women, boundless reassurance speaks through him as a father, and his integrity walks by his side as an eternal friend in every walk of life.

* * * * * * * *

In his daily practice of stability and forbearance, in order to anchor himself in his unshakeable essence, he reflects on the following questions;

- ✓ Do I depend upon my joyous memories of the past for my fulfillment, or am I the grateful but equanimous observer of my past?
- ✓ How affected am I by the fluctuations of my environment?
- ✓ Do I feel anger or frustration in the face of setbacks, delays or adversities?
- ✓ How aligned am I towards my principles, and how determined am I to live simple-heartedly?

28.SELF-AWARENESS, HIS PATHWAY

"Atmajnanan vidurjnanam jnanayanyani yani tu.
Tani jnana vabhasani sarasya neva bodhanat."[9]
[Self-knowledge is real knowledge, all other knowledge is a mere shadow of self-knowledge. Other knowledge will not lead to realization of the truth.]

"To know the Cognitive Faculty means to merge in it. The Cognitive Faculty is the witnessing entity of the functioning of that stage of the mind that is the subtlest feeling of existence. It is like a salt doll trying to fathom the depth of the ocean, and in the process becoming one with the ocean itself; it could not return and tell others the story of how it felt while fathoming the ocean. This sort of becoming one with the ocean while trying to fathom it is termed 'self-knowledge', and all other knowledge in the worldly sphere is not real knowledge, it is just the umbra and penumbra of 'real' knowledge.

Shiva propounded, "Atmamokshartham jagathitaya cha" [Self-realization and service to humanity] as the two simultaneous paths of spiritual practice to liberate oneself from the bondages of human limitations (egoism, Karma and illusion). Subjective knowledge, the knowledge of the 'I' as captured in the ancient texts, helps human beings reach the golden line of self-realization. Attaining self-knowledge through subjective knowledge, such human beings will move towards their final destination, the Supreme Benevolence, and merge in the sweetest ocean of bliss for eternity."

(Adopted from Namah Shivaya Shantaya by Shr. Shr. Anandamurti)

* * * * * * * *

Man is like flowing water. To keep its radiance and sparkle, to keep its fragrance and clarity, water must flow, for it must sing its melodies, it must script its refrains, it must carve its cobblestones; this it achieves in its effortless flow. It is the same for man. His quest for greater self-awareness brings him further in the act called life. His quest takes him beyond the physical, it brings him closer to his purpose, it ignites his passion, it awakens his knowing. In his discovery of meaning, he inspires commitment, he creates attraction. In his recognition of his infinite potential, he whistles in bliss, and in his knowing of his infinite nature, he expands consciousness.

When water stops to flow, it loses its smile. It loses its shine. It turns mouldy. It starts to smell foul and it has become the dumping place for flotsam and jetsam. Stagnant water tells the story of man living life against his very nature, a story of not having allowed himself to live his fullest might, a story of force applied to resist his very destiny.

When a man lets himself be left behind in life, it becomes visible in the mirror of the universe around him. He notices that he is too young for his life, he is too limited for his age, he walks in shoes too big to fit him. The world around him seems out of place, and the voices around him tell him that he has not caught up with where life ought to be. Meaninglessness becomes his constant companion, and he lives in the fallacy that emptiness is peace.

Through every generation, mankind has questioned the virtues of the path of self-awareness, for what the eyes in him cannot see, the rational within him cannot conceive. The passing parade of the worldly life with its frills and frivolous, that which is tickling to his sensorial self, that which is nearest to his existential experience, it has appealed to his cause-and-effect mind. So why look beyond into the unknown, he has asked.

He who is in pursuit of self-awareness, he will recognize his true place in the world, that he is not above it, as modern man erroneously thinks, but he is of it. When man recognizes this truth, he falls into harmony with his surroundings, that like a raft in a river, he becomes of the river than separate from it. In this knowing can he access his *Dharma*, that innate nature of his, for through him he is connected to his assignment in life. His constant endeavour must be to remain connected to his inner voice, that truest voice that is the echo of the Absolute, and he must choose to live in alignment with it, for he has it in his choice to live in alignment. Therein lies the deepest joy of man, the joy that finds its origin in his purpose, bringing meaning to his 'being' and 'doing', flooding him with effulgent love towards all, making the losses bearable and the troubles affordable.

His self-awareness serves him to accept with confidence that he is a reflection of the Divine, that he is an echo of the Absolute, that his life is preordained to be, rather than a quirky happenstance, that he is the carrier of that higher cause that is ordained for fruition of Nature's greatest mission, and in that knowing the Mature Masculine rejoices in his self. To believe in Nature is to believe in himself, for he is a product of Its divine notion. There from comes the Mature Masculine's innocent curiosity and awe of his own meaning, akin to a child's wonderment of his first steps; that the Mature Masculine can risk curiosity, wonderment, spontaneous delight, or any experience that reveals the human spirit.

He who is the explorer of self-knowledge is one who can smile freely in wonderment of the world, give profusely to the other, access the infinite possibilities that lie at every step of his journey, experience the full length of his gratitude for what he has become, for he has traversed through many lives, shifting consciousness, to form into who he is today. The Mature Masculine has shattered his casing of illegitimate fear within which he has found himself trapped, the fear that is the exertion of his ego, the fear that is the construct of the mind, the fear that limits him in his fullest expression, the fear that chokes the easiest flow of his abundant love, the fear that had made it nearly impossible for him to previously make time for his true mission; for illegitimate fear is limited to man's human contours, that which is constantly seeking to legitimize the illusions of his wakefulness reality. The Mature Masculine has found his powers to script and sculpt his path in life. He who walks his road of self-awareness, has come to the realization that his journey towards greater self-awareness is his journey towards oneness with the Infinite, and his every thought and intention acts as a cobblestone on his path, making his journey an accessory of his choices.

Self-awareness is not the study of history, physics, literature or art. All these faculties can give man a sense of who he is not, and also promote his well-being in his physical and material reality. However, they can only take him as far as the gateway to his subtle inner realm, but only as far as that.

Nor can man discover the 'I' within him by learning about others. That will be similar to studying a shadow to learn about the object. Studying the shadow, man might get a sense of the *gross* elements of the object, like its contour or size, but the *subtle* attributes of the object shall elude him. The shadow of the object will not lend him an understanding of the colour, the smell, the fragrance or the texture of the object itself.

Psychoanalytic tests illuminate the functions and expressions of man's mind; they help him understand the pre-conditioned nature of his mind, and illuminate upon its performing. Habits have solidified within him to become his pre-conditioned nature and he acts out of these pre-conditionings in his day to day interactions. These tests may give him a sense of how his mind operates; however, man must go into himself, go beyond the mind into the non-physical realm to understand the real 'I' within him, that which is the finest and truest about him. While the intellect may hold his hand and bring him as far as the doorstep to self-awareness, he must relinquish the intellect beyond the frontier of self-knowledge, in order to surrender into the experience of intuitive knowing of the union of self with the Self. In his complete surrender to the unknown space of consciousness within, in his fullest devotion to the truth of its existence within man, he lives the bliss of the 'I' within himself.

Many left-handed *Tantric* practitioners indulge in the use of psychedelic substances in order to access the bliss associated with the experience of 'I' within them. While such use of substances is but a poor substitute to the experience of 'I' within oneself, and does not help man develop the self-awareness of the 'I' within him, it does give a glimpse of the bliss in store for man in that melding.

It is said to have known from Shiva;
"Vidyaya tu pramuchyaté"

[Knowledge* leads to liberation.]
(*: Here is meant self-knowledge)

The Mature Masculine is aware that in surrendering into the field of consciousness that permeates through all beings, the field that is built upon love, the field that is built for joy, his journey begins by encountering those *Tamasic* (dark) forces that reside within him in the form of his traumas. He must slay those dragons, not through any act of violence, but by gently accepting and embracing those traumas as part of his *Karma*, accumulated through years and lifetimes of existence. Patiently and valiantly, trudging through that tunnel, the Mature Masculine will master those dark forces, to be freed to glimpse that 'I' within himself and to experience the bliss of being in one with all that is.

Man commonly experiences the full force of his self-knowing through the effective use of perception and inference, and through the well-discriminated embrace of authoritative sources.

Perception involves inner knowing, opening those inner doors behind which is contained all the knowing that defines the universe, the knowing which forms the reference for Nature's existence. The Mature Masculine taps into his inner knowing by connecting with that which is already within, his inner source, through the process of meditation. This he must, for his conscious mind is limited in its capacity of understanding new truths without the inherent bias of his previous knowledge. His knowing is his truth, for the limited conscious mind of man can grasp only that to which it has been exposed. The truth of anything external to man cannot be understood by he who has not found his own truth within, for it is in reference to his own truth that he can realize the truth of all that is external to him. And when man views objects without understanding his own truth, objects simply remain as transitory impressions in his mind.

Inference involves thinking and recollection; recollection of all that is already resident within man. To infer truth that is own to him, truth about his very being, man must recollect all that is subtle within. When he can crawl out of the pit hole of dogma, and leverage his unlimited capacity of *Viveka*, the power of discrimination, like a drill penetrating matter, man can descend towards increasing subtlety. Shiva, who persisted with His journey of self-realization did, through the process of synthesis, enter the subtle world of His mind, until He found that which is eternal and immortal about Him.

Authoritative sources which remind man of his authentic essence are plentiful, he has at his disposal many texts originating from many indigenous civilizations and ancient religions. The Mature Masculine who seeks self-knowledge, with a discriminating and rationalistic mind, with sensitive regard to his own observations and intuition, steeps his learning from such sources. Thus he realizes the true meaning of his soul, and feels the exceeding joy of self-awareness. This was the forte of Shiva, in whose life example man has experienced that great truth, which is the same truth that governs man and every other entity in the entire universe.

* * * * * * * *

To re-enforce his daily practice of self-awareness, the Mature Masculine as himself the following questions;

- ✓ Am I stagnant in my self development or am I expanding self-awareness everyday?
- ✓ Today, what is the one thing I must do in order to expand my self-awareness?
- ✓ Is there more to me than what I see in the mirror?
- ✓ How differently do I see the truth of external things, as I continue finding my own truth within myself?

29.RADIATING HIS BENEVOLENT SPIRIT

"Thou art the ocean of mercy,
Thou art giver of boons,
You blessed Arjuna and Bana,
You swallowed the poison".

(Sarvalinga Stava).

In one of the mythological tales, the gods and demons were engaged in a relentless war. As the gods were being outnumbered, they decided that only 'Amrit', the nectar of immortality lying deep within the ocean could save the gods from extinction. To churn the ocean and extract the 'Amrit', the gods decided to pool their strength in with the demons. A truce was arrived at under the condition that the gods and the demons would share the 'Amrit'.

It is said so in the tale that the gods and the demons used a mountain as the churning rod and the world serpent as the churning rope. As the gods and the demons churned the ocean, many priceless treasures were recovered from the bottom of the ocean. The king of gods, 'Indra', appropriated the celestial elephant that surfaced during the churning, Vishnu, known as the god of preservation, took as his consort 'Lakshmi', the goddess of wealth as she appeared from the ocean, and the gods took possession of many other treasures. As the caustic world poison surfaced during the churning, threatening all of creation, the gods and demons fled. Shiva, the Benevolent One, the one who is beyond self-interest, drank willingly the poison in order to save all of creation.

Countless are the mythological and real life stories from Shiva's life, where it is narrated of those with their twisted ways, who sucked the elixir of His benevolence and large-heartedness. He knew, but chose not to change His ways. Thus the noble personality, the remover of all worldly afflictions, He was lovingly called 'Kalyanamukha' (supreme benevolence).

* * * * * * * *

When man relates to his worldly existence as his ultimate reality, every faculty of his being is aimed at propping up his material existence. His material welfare becomes his paramount pursuit and the unconscious driver of his actions. In this misplaced reality lies the origin of man's fears, he remains consumed by the fear of survival, he fears losing belongingness in life, and he fears losing identity.

However, when man recognizes the higher meaning of his existence - for every man is endowed with a life purpose that is greater than himself - his 'being' and 'doing' are not bound by his illegitimate fears, instead bound by his abundant love. In meaning he finds his passion, and passion becomes the ice upon which he slides forward effortlessly. The Mature Masculine lives out his passion, hence his love expresses plentifully in his giving, for that only which is given in love is given truly, that there is no pain in its loss, rather the bliss of giving. He is not consumed by rewards, his acts are not governed by fears, his ego is not in yearning for association. Neither is he a victim of circumstances, nor has he trapped himself in his existential, belongingness or identity fears, for these fears are triggered by the illusion of his material existence. In his act of giving, the Mature Masculine is not bound by selfish outcomes, for when man gives with intent to self-enhance himself, the act of giving binds him further to the beneficiary. Like an animal on quicksand, he sinks fast into the egoistic trap of artificial indebtedness. The Mature Masculine gives not out of compulsion, rather of his own volition. That is a sign of his self-mastery.

When man is not a victim of his inner or outer circumstances, he turns into a being with abundance, for such is the nature of Nature. Man with a pure intention **is** plentiful when he **feels** plentiful. What has manifested internally within his being automatically manifests externally, not vice versa. The science of Nature conspires to bring under man's ownership that which he has manifested internally, for all that man wants is already available. However, against the will of every cell in his body, the unknowing man labours tirelessly to serve the calling of his fears, slogging day and night to build fences of security against every conceivable setback in life, for the illusion of man beckons that he must shape an external reality that is misaligned with his inner reality. As a result he is often left wondering about the impermanence of the fruits of his labour. When man has not first internally manifested the abundance that he externally owns, like dry sand hissing and slipping through his fingers, like tents blown away in desert storms, the fruits of his effortful labour leave his possession.

From the place of abundance, man's act of giving becomes effortless, for he has not less as he gives. On the contrary, his act of giving further replenishes his inner treasury by compounding his abundance with the fresh joy of giving.

Man must recognize his part in the universe, that without him knowing he is in constant exchange with his surroundings. That all rivers flow into the ocean, that when the river is one with the ocean it loses its identity; that all waves are part of the ocean, that once the wave crashes it has lost its individual form. That at every level of the mind – of which his body is a part of – he is in continuous engagement with his environment and beyond. The Mature Masculine realizes this very truth upon which Nature functions, that to take and keep for himself at the expense of another is to become separate from the whole, and to give to another is but to give to himself. Therefore, man who has been deprived of his right to give is absolutely bankrupt. This ownership, which is the only thing he can call his own, which if lost, is also a loss to his entire meaning. The desire the Mature Masculine has to give is really the desire of the Absolute acting through him.

It is said,
"Tyaktena bhunjithah"
[Thou shall gain by giving away.]

All giving gives back. All benevolence returns in higher sums. This is the law of Nature. However, man must give not with self-enhancing outcomes in mind, for in that longing he meets his defeat. He has succumbed to the forces of his ego, his ego pulling him in self-reinforcing ways, and he has enlivened the illusion of his separateness from those of others. Being in service to another with the expectation of receiving something in return, is man being oblivious to the truth that it the nature of Nature to close the loop and reward any act of giving and any gesture of service.

The Mature Masculine – in his act of giving - carries within him the aspiration for outcomes, outcomes that rise higher than himself to caress the receiver. In his words and deeds is hidden his intention to heal, and to help the receiver of his service learn to love, for in his offering is the union that frees all beings from fear. There is no urgency though, no haste in the Mature Masculine's search for outcomes, no desire, no effort to be seen, only perfection of his calm, only quietness of his appearance, only equanimity from craving, for the Mature Masculine is aware that the sacrifice that brings meaning to his existence, the sacrifice by which he attains his fulfilment is not a sacrifice after all, it is simply him living the bliss of his *Dharma*, his highest purpose. Like a candle melting down into extinction in its act of fulfilling its purpose of existence, sacrifice is its own reward for the Mature Masculine, for he is joyfully intent upon the radiance of his life lived on purpose, rather than the sacrifice involved.

Benevolence is the act of gifting his benefit of doubt to the other. It involves the simple-heartedness of man to see the goodness in the other, and to use that goodness as his anchor to relate to the other. The Mature Masculine uses his power of discrimination to recognize the circumstances and motivation that make others act in ungodly ways, that it is not the nature of any being to live, think, speak or act in evil, for every being is constructed of goodness. There from originates his benefit of doubt.

Free from fear - the fears of survival, lack of belongingness, or losing identity – all beings are engaged in the magnification of love, that free from the clutches of the ego, every being lives in intention of welfare.

This is the truth behind the popular chant hailing the very presence of Shiva within each man;
"Chidanandarupah Sivoham Sivoham"

[I am auspiciousness, I am Shiva of the form of knowledge and bliss.]

This very auspiciousness that is true within every man, it is that which we notice in our worldly life each time we see the Mature Masculine step forward in defence of humanity's highest goodness. He who we know as the Mature Masculine is he who reveres our collective goodness, and who lives in service of bringing to the surface that collective goodness that on occasions lie buried under the debris of the ego.

The Mature Masculine exhibits his benevolence also through his gift of allowing. He is aware that life is but a canoe in a flowing stream, that its water will take his life on its course to his destiny as long as he would allow the stream do its deed. As is man made to liberate himself, the liberation that comes from following his own pious inner voice, so is every being in Nature created to express its innateness through its *Dharma* (its purpose of existence). To judge otherwise is to dishonour the knowingness of other beings, an insult to *Parama Purusha* (Supreme Consciousness), a reflection of which all beings – including himself - are. Man who withholds such gift of allowing, letting not the other flourish in its own grace, is he who is bankrupt in love and compassion. He gets afflicted by the malady of resisting what is, thus stealing from the other his birth right to fulfil his purpose. When man renounces any desire to control, instead offer the gift of space to the other to become one with himself, to blossom into his fullest grandeur and to fulfil his purpose, then man is in practice of allowing. Only the renounced can truly give, for *Seva* – the act of selfless giving - is ensconced in renunciation. This truth expands the understanding that true giving is not solely the forte of monks - those who practice renunciation - rather it is applicable for any from all walks of life, including a householder.

*   *   *   *   *   *   *   *

In the daily practice of living his innate benevolence, the Mature Masculine uses the following questions to recognize for himself the true nature of his giving;

- ✓ That which I am giving, am I giving with no reward or recognition in mind?
- ✓ That which I am giving now, am I giving out of compulsion, or am I giving out of my own volition?
- ✓ Am I giving out of my deep sense of service, and to heal, and to unite people in love?
- ✓ Do I feel abundant within about everything I have, or do I live from a scarcity paradigm?
- ✓ Am I allowing others to blossom into their natural fullness, or do I control their development?

30.HUMILITY – LETTING LOVE FLOW

"Ahamkara patanesya mulam"
[Arrogance precedes a fall]
(Shavaite proverb)

It is said that once the 'Devas' (gods) became puffed up with victory over the 'Asuras' (demons). They wrongly took the success to be the result of their own valour and prowess. Shiva wanted to teach them a lesson in humility, so He appeared in front of them as an endless entity, the beginning and end of which were not visible.

The gods wanting to find out the identity of this Form sent 'Agni' - the god of fire - over. The Endless Entity asked 'Agni', "What is your name and power?" 'Agni' replied, "I am Agni, and I can burn up the entire universe in a minute." The Endless Entity placed before 'Agni' a dry blade of grass and asked him to burn it. Unable to burn it, 'Agni' disappeared in shame.

The gods next sent 'Vayu' - the wind god - to discover the identity of the Endless Entity. As 'Vayu' approached the Endless Entity, He enquired again, "Who are you and what is your power?" 'Vayu' replied, "I am Vayu, the wind god, and I can blow away the whole world in a minute." Again the Endless Entity placed another blade of grass, this time in front of 'Vayu' and asked him to blow it away. Try as hard as he may, 'Vayu' could not move the blade an inch. He also returned back in shame.

Last of all came 'Indra' - the king of the gods – himself. When he arrived at the place, the Endless Entity had vanished, and standing there was

Shiva revealing to 'Indra' the true identity of the Endless Entity, being that of Himself. 'Indra' felt humbled.

*   *   *   *   *   *   *   *

Self-realization man must practice, for only then will he know his place in the universe. Rather than consider himself an isolated entity in the cosmic landscape, rather than expound his superiority in Nature's hierarchy, the Mature Masculine, who is on his path of self-realization, recognizes himself as another cog in the wheel, a wheel which is composed of billions of other known entities that have been assembled together to perform the cosmic orchestra. He is as integral to the scheme of Nature as all other entities are, all being crucial links in the chain, parts of the cycle of Nature. Only he who gets overcome by the vanity of his ego forgets his rightful place in the scheme of the universe.

Self-realization entails the recognition that man's reality in his wakefulness state is an illusion, that the gross body that he experiences in his wakeful state is transient, that in the wakeful state object cannot exist without the subject. In the wakefulness reality, man exists only in the eyes of a witness, and when the witness turns his head away, man becomes non-existent in the reality of the witness. Man may be conscious of himself, but for others he is merely a figment of imagination when he is absent from their presence. Imagination however exists in the dream realm, in the subtle body of the imaginer. And when the imaginer shuts his imagination off, man becomes non-existent in the subtle reality of the witness as well. Hence in the wakefulness or dream reality man's existence requires the subject, or the witness; that in spite of his pomp and misplaced notion of his own importance, he is insignificant. That the unlearned man who lives the fallacy of his material existence shall always remain at the mercy of another for his existence, however big or small, however rich or poor, however learned or ignorant, however insensitive or compassionate the other may be. In this realization he must find his humility.

The Mature Masculine aspires to awaken humanity from its darkness, and he longs to lift it out of its self-perpetuated lack of fulfilment. He notices with equanimity and humility the complexities his brethren have created for themselves, and he is a conscious observer of their aimless wanderings through life compounded by their own meaninglessness. He observes that they have closed their doors and have their windows locked, choosing to remain where they are, lest the power of love should penetrate their walls and lift them into a higher space where their foothold may not be as firm as in their material world. Though the Mature Masculine despairs not, it is through his humility that he accepts that all beings are equal cogs in the same wheel of the universe, that all beings are intricately woven together in an energetic web of interrelationships, that all beings are of the same substance and same space, that it is the same consciousness that permeates through all beings.

The Mature Masculine has surrendered himself in service to others in the self-realization that he is born a humble instrument for the broader welfare. Therefore he has dedicated himself to the betterment of all beings, simultaneously recognizing with humility that he will remain an eternal student of life. He is joyous in his aspiration to break off his shackles of ignorance and expand his understanding of all there is. Through his learning he becomes the tool for social change, though never compelled by the slightest need for recognition, for the Mature Masculine has shun all vanity of performance.

The Mature Masculine is aware that the only entity under his control is himself, including his inherent thoughts and the reality that he has consciously and unconsciously shaped for himself. From this knowingness, he chooses to live a radiating example to those around him – not because he is driven by the motivation of impressing upon his brethren his virtues – rather recognizing with humility that the unique blessing of life that he is endowed with, is with the purpose of living his highest, most divine self.

Man must know his place in the universe. It is only the naïve man who believes that the reflection of the sun seen in the pond in which he lives is the sun itself. He might try to live his life by himself, isolated and out of alignment with Nature, having to exert force to lead life, but without the backdrop of the Universe – of which he is a part of – his force will not reflect his infinite power. Try as hard as he may, the reflection of the sun in the pond in which he lives will not offer him the heat to keep the cycle of life flowing, and the light to illuminate his journey of life.

In his haughty belief of his own might, in his separateness from the Absolute and all other beings, in his creation of a world of his own where he has enthroned himself the king, he minimizes himself into a mere mortal, his life degenerates into a mere sensorial pursuit guided by his ego's craving, and his infinite fails to radiate. It takes an awakened man to dethrone himself from the centre of his own little world, to accept that there is only one world – the world of the Absolute - of which he is a part of.

So it is said in mythology of the creations of Shiva;

"Ayam loko nasti para iti mani"
[This world exists, there is no other.]

Humility is the embrace of this truth by the Mature Masculine, the wholeness of which he is gladly a part of, the world to which he belongs, finding his humble place in the grander scheme of the Absolute. For, in the process he only trades his individual 'I' for something greater, and his pettiness centred on his 'I' is transformed into vastness. No more has he to fight to keep his place in the cosmic landscape; it is secure for him by the immortal right of his soul.

Human nature is so feeble that it is helpless in helping itself towards self-realization. Man's ultimate self-realization is beyond the scope of unassisted learning. If he is to escape from his darkness that his human self holds, and reach the perfection for which he is preordained, he needs a transforming force.

Man who is filled with grandiose chokes his learning, and his progress on his path towards *Parama Purusha* (Supreme Consciousness) comes to a halt. He banishes from his mind its natural yearning for its truth, further compounding his ignorance. Being a dynamic entity, movement is the law that governs his existence; thus when he is not surging forward he is sinking backward along the path of degradation and eventual downfall. All his intellectual abilities, all his swaggering and boasting comes to naught.

He for whom humility is a premise of learning, he is wedded to the truth propounded by Shiva;
"Acharya devo bhava"
[Be one to whom teacher is the divine.]

The Mature Masculine is he who realizes the truth that when he gets rid of his pride of self, he comes into his true inheritance. Every encounter in life is his inheritance, encounters designed to be his teacher. He who has – with humility - surrendered into the joy of learning lets no truth be neglected, lets no virtue be neglected, lets no welfare be neglected, lets no prosperity be neglected, lets no study of teaching be neglected, lets no duty be neglected.

While the existence of the ego is natural to all manifested beings, the expression of egoism is the demon of the masculine. Such man is dependent upon the experiences, circumstances, people and objects around him for meaning, and his ego relies on the relentless pursuit of approval of others. Achievement becomes the mantra of his life, and all his actions are tuned towards this purpose. And as he frees himself from the traps of egoism, he discovers that his job cannot bind him, his common interest groups cannot hold him down, and he feels freed from any activity that he undertakes in order to unconsciously prop up his identity. All his 'doing' will become meritorious acts for the solidarity of the world that he lives in.

Ego serves man in his self-preservation of his human existence, this it does through the experience of fears, some legitimate some not from a human light. His body wants to remain, his psyche wants to thrive, and the ego is the agent that strives to ensure that. The expression of the soul – on the other hand - is love, the love that aspires to liberate man from the bondages he has created for himself. Love is that which elevates him from the limitations of the body and the psyche, to bring him towards oneness with Spirit. He who has sacrificed his soul to the unruly pursuit of power and the drunkenness of status, he whose ego has inclined him to the vanity of exhibitionism and his debilitating passion of profit-making, he has foregone his own freedom to experience the wonderment of life. When man tries to raise himself to eminence by pushing aside all others, to achieve a distinction by which he prides himself to be more than everybody else, he is disconnected from that love which is innate to him. He is alienated from the Supreme Consciousness, for whatever he treasures for himself separates him from others.

As discussed earlier, man's place is among all beings, not above them, nor below. In recognizing and reconciling this, he has become of truth and he has availed of peace; he has proclaimed his perfection by becoming conscious of the spirit of unity that lies within all.

This is what is meant when it is said in the ancient truths;
"Ahamkaram evapyeti yo ham-karam evastam eti"
[He who absorbs the self-sense, in him does the self-sense reach extinction.]

Like with everything in Nature, man may lack symmetry or proportion, refinement or sharpness, however that holds true for all creations. What makes an artist's rendering of Nature so perfect is his capture of the imperfections. What makes his art perfect is not the perfect contours and contrast, rather the exquisite blend of the beautiful and the ugly, the good and the bad, the small and the big, the tall and the short, the bright and the dark. The same holds true for the Mature Masculine. Once away from his own judgment and self-condemnation, his humility can come around to fully accept who he is. When the Mature Masculine admits to that imperfection without self-castigation, to shrug his shoulders and accept what is, then he becomes of that place where love incessantly flows through him.

*   *   *   *   *   *   *   *

The Mature Masculine uses the following questions as his gauge in his daily practice of humility;

- ✓ How much is my self-worth dependent upon others' views or opinions of me?
- ✓ Do I feel superior to other people and other beings?
- ✓ How do I remind myself that I am not the centre of my own world, rather a part of a larger world?
- ✓ Do I feel like I have learned everything that I needed to know, and there is no further wisdom that can serve my existence further?
- ✓ Am I driven by my need for status, power and approval, or by my longing for union with others in love?

31.EPILOGUE

Transformation begins with awareness, creating awareness in man towards the essence of mature masculinity being the intention behind this book. As man surrenders into this awareness and continues - in deep devotion - to remain in awareness, his pathway presents itself. Though the eventual destination is the same for all, every man has his own pathway of transformation, and it is each passionate man's prerogative to seek it for himself.

There is no defined recipe for man's own path of transformation, however he is endowed with a magnificent internal compass called the intuition. Penetrating through all the layers of the mind, it is through the intuition that the one in man threads its course towards the one in All; thus intuition is all-knowing and has access to the Infinite to bring forth to man the wisdom and knowingness he needs in order to continue on his journey of transformation. He must remember that he can never fully possess his highest being merely at the intellectual level. It has to be experienced, and this experience involves the heart; it involves devotion. And that is what is called for from the Mature Masculine, to surrender himself with unshakeable faith and disciplined devotion; this discipline man has to go through to elevate himself to the highest he can be, the Mature Masculine.

Such transformation does not mean for man to turn into someone who he is not. On the contrary, it is the invitation to come home to who he really is; away from the layers of roles that he has played and the masks that he has worn through his years of sculpting. This is what is meant when the sages have said so of Shiva;

"Iha chet avedit atha satyamasti"
[To know him in this life is to be true.]

What worked for me may or may not work for another. It is in my daily practice of realizing and affirming the presence of the mature masculine within me that I experience my fullest joy. The Cosmic Force has benevolently brought to me every day all the resources required for me along my path of growth. I accepted with grace and gratitude the coaches, teachers, friends, literature, encounters and experiences that have this far appeared alongside my path. I look back and recognize that all these resources appeared at precise moments and at the right place.

As I look backwards, the dots seem to connect. Like a drink gratefully accepted by the runner with a parched throat climbing uphill exhausted under the scorching sun, I have gleefully accepted that which has been offered to me. I am awestruck at the *Lila* (divine playfulness) of the Supreme in orchestrating my inner process. It is my constant endeavour to patiently and resolutely trudge forever on this blissful path of self-realization, a journey that will reach its completion only when I am fully and eternally in oneness with my mature masculine self.

In my daily prayer, I hold the same passionate intention for every man to be in truth, truth that is born out of his union with his mature masculine self, for when he is with his heart and mind the mature masculine who dwells within, he is assured of everlasting bliss. It is then that we call him *Mahatma*, the great soul.

The universe is an echo, for it expresses man's inner truth through its outer movements. It acts as a screen upon which man's every thought, word and deed leave bountiful signs for him to see, learn from and grow in his voyage of increased refinement towards his mature masculine self. The feminine, being part of the universal force, also serves as a profound indicator of how aligned a man is with his mature masculine self. When man realizes that he is much more than at present he seems to be, and he grows aware of that which he is yet to be, and he lives in the knowing that it is within him to be the greatest that he can be, then the unconscious admiration, respect, willingness to surrender, attraction or love that exudes from the feminine, be it through his spouse, mother, daughter, sister, friends or acquaintances, inflames his process of transformation. That is the law of Nature.

I wish every inspired reader his or her bliss of self-realization. I am reminded that each one of us has the choice to shape his or her future, and that we have the power to alter our destiny. If you are a man, may your life be an inspiring commentary of the Mature Masculine, and if you are a woman, may you be the noble champion of bringing back men to their Mature Masculine self.

TAT TVAM ASI (you are That).

SELECTED REFERENCES

1. Autobiography of a Yogi: Paramahansa Yogananda
2. Be as You Are: The Teachings of Sri Ramana Maharshi: Sri Ramana Maharshi and David Godman
3. Conquest of Mind: Sri Swami Sivananda
4. Creative Unity: Rabindranath Tagore
5. Encountering Saivism: The Deity, the Milieu, the Entourage: Nilima Chitgopekar
6. Experiencing Siva: Fred Clothey and Bruce Long
7. Hinduism, A Religion to Live: Oxford University Press
8. Lord Siva and His Worship: Sri Swami Sivananda
9. Namah Shivaya Shantaya: Shrii Shrii Anandamurti
10. Pashupatinath: T.R. Majupuria and I. Majupuria
11. Pushpadantas Shivamahimna Stotram: V.V.B.Rama Rao
12. Sadhana: Rabindranath Tagore
13. Secret of the Veda, New U.S. Edition: Aurobindo
14. Shiva: An Introduction: Devdutt Pattanaik
15. Shiva: Shakti M. Gupta
16. Shiva: The Wild God of Power and Ecstasy: Wolf-Dieter Storl
17. Significance of the Tantric Tradition: Kamalakar Mishra
18. Siva: Eye of the Storm: Lakshmi Lal
19. Siva Sutras: The Yoga of Supreme Identity: Jaideva Singh
20. Siva: The Erotic Ascetic: Wendy Doniger O'Flaherty
21. Speaking of Siva: Translated by A.K. Ramanujan
22. Sri Rudram and Chamakam: Rajagopala Aiyar
23. The book of Shiva: Deepak Chopra
24. The book of Shiva: Namita Gokhale
25. The Esoteric Philosophy Of Tantra (Shiva Sanhita): Translation from Srischandra Basu

26. The Holy Vedas; Rig Veda, Yajur Veda, Sama Veda, Atharva Veda: Dipavali Debroy
27. The Indian Theogony: Brahma, Vishnu and Siva: Sukumari Bhattacharji
28. The Presence of Shiva: Stella Kramrisch
29. The Principal Upanishad: S. Radhakrishnan
30. The Seven Spiritual Laws of Success: Deepak Chopra
31. The Tantras: An Overview: Swami Samarpanananda
32. The Upanishads: Breath of the Eternal: Swami Prabhavanada and Frederick Manchester
33. The Wisdom of Tantra: Acharya Vedaprajinananda Avadhuta
34. The Years of Awakening: Krishnamurti
35. Wisdom and Mystical Verses of Sanor: Dada Shambhushivananda